Testimonies

God's Unfolding Miracles

by Maxine Williams Wright

RoseDog Books

PITTSBURGH, PENNSYLVANIA 15238

RoseDog Books
585 Alpha Drive
Suite 103
Pittsburgh, PA 15238
Visit our website at *www.rosedogbookstore.com*

ISBN: 978-1-6386-7417-7
eISBN: 978-1-6386-7518-1

Table of Contents

DEDICATION TO MY...

Parents
Thomas Williams & Rosie L. Booker Williams

Grandparents
Bennie Booker & Alma Jean Hardeman-Booker & Lula Bridges-Booker
Thomas Williams, Sr. & Emma Graham

Sons
Marriem A. Armstrong & Austin T. Wright

Grandchildren
Marquise Martin & Chelsea Coleman & Kelsey Coleman
Kahmil Patton & Style Awar Wright Brown
Legend Amore Clarke

Siblings
Lula M. Booker Golden & Robert E. Williams
Thomas P. Williams & Timothy Jackson

Other Family Members
Aunts & Uncles
Nieces & Nephews & Cousins & Sisters in Law

Educational Institutions
Northside High School & Tennessee State University
Morris Brown College

Special Acknowledgements

Witnesses

Andrew Booker

Catrina Ravenel

Cossetta Taylor

Dianne Coggins

Dorothy D. Hart

Ernest L. Foster

Marvin Baldwin, Jr.

Patricia M. Goins

Paula G Voice

Rev. Leela Waller

Rev. Teronda P. Hamilton

T.S. Edwards

Wanda J. Booker-Wade

Willie Arnez La'Monta Booker

Special *Thanks* to all that **have** encouraged, **supported** and prayed!

The Vision

I was inspired to write this book of Testimonies (God's Unfolding Miracles) to share life changing moments. We often share our life changing moments with immediate family and friends. We need to give God the Glory and spread the good news He is still working on our behalf. This book consists of actual miracles, acts of The Most High God! The testimonies will make an unbeliever a believer, give hope to the hopeless, and provide light in the midst of darkness. The witnesses have shared their intimate moments with you, for you!

This is the day God planted His vision in my spirit. A day to remember! On Sunday, September 20, 2020, I heard a sermon from John 20:30-31 titled "He's Still Moving." The minister spoke about the miracles performed in the Old Testament and the miracles Jesus performed in the New Testament. At the end of his sermon he shared his testimony and what he had gone through seven months prior to the sermon. He shared about the lesions on both legs from his ankles to his waist. He shared how he went to his doctor thinking it was leprosy since the lesions appeared like slashes made with a razor. The doctor diagnosed him with Hodgkin's Lymphoma Disease after the biopsy and he shared how the doctor informed him time was running out because soon the lesions would cover his entire body. The minister stated, "My wife and I began to fast and pray, pray and fast. I was sleep one day and felt a warmness that covered my whole body. I jumped up and ran into the bathroom, pulled down my pajamas to look in a full length mirror. I was healed!

There were no blemishes on my body. My wife is a witness. My legs looked better than they did when I was 25. God is able. I'm here to announce God is still moving! There's nothing too hard for God!"

After I heard his testimony my spirit became restless. I didn't know what was going on. I had planned to work on another project and couldn't focus. The testimony got all under my skin and wouldn't leave me alone. No matter what I did, it wouldn't get out of my head. I was consumed with thoughts about testimonies. Finally, I heard these exact words, "I want you to share my miracles." I didn't understand what to do. In fact, how was I supposed to do that? Then I heard it again...

Obedience is better than sacrifice.

After I gathered my thoughts, an idea to do what God wanted me to do became visible. I prayed and asked Him to lead me to the right people. Some faces surfaced immediately, some came later. Then I started sending text messages and making phone calls. Some didn't think I was serious and some said okay and weren't serious. Some didn't respond to my message. Some felt my spirit and were convinced immediately. Some had delayed reactions. Some I chose were unable due to other obligations. Some just didn't have an interest. Some were on another assignment from God. Everything is not for everyone and things are in due season. Also I prayed and asked The Most High God to remove me, to work through me, and to guide me. Then I stepped out on His word.

The process was in motion to implement the project. I was amazed and grateful that The Most High God selected me for this assignment. One evening I spoke with a person I had asked to participate and he voiced concerns about the terms of the agreement. I didn't get a chance to explain the terms before he expressed another concern. He stated I wasn't writing a book, I was only editing stories from others. When the conversation was over I sat still for a moment and heard these words whispered to me, "I want you to write comments after each testimony." I had not planned that at all. I was only going to share and edit testimonies from others including my testimonies which was the original message I received. And who was I to make comments after someone's life changing moments? But if I needed to do it I would. I didn't have any ideas about what to write, how to write, or how it would be received. When I wrote my first inspirational thought, I knew it did not come from me. I allowed The Most High God to use me and He will get the glory. God did work it out.

Obedience is better than sacrifice. God will transpose opposition. Stay focused! Will you allow The Most High God to use you? Get ready to share your miracles. God is indeed moving!

"I Pray with open eyes,
    I Speak beyond boundary lines,
        I Write in cyberspace,
            I Dream of metaphoric rhymes,
                I… P.S.W.D. with the love I have in me,
                    with the harmony of the Trinity."

Psalm 46:1-3

"God is our refuge and strength, an ever-present help in trouble. Therefore we will not fear, though the earth gives way and the mountains fall into the heart of the sea, though its waters roar and foam and the mountains quake with their surging."

Maxine Williams Wright

CHAPTER 1

Enough

MAXINE WILLIAMS WRIGHT
Marietta, Georgia

My second husband was a military man stationed at the NSA Mid South Naval Base in Millington, TN. I was introduced to him, we dated and married within a year then relocated to Washington, D.C. My mother begged me not to take my four year old son and place him with a man he did not know. But I wanted to care for my son because he was my responsibility not the responsibility of my mom and dad. I married him to give my son a father figure and he made promises I couldn't resist. The two years we lived in Washington, D.C. were not good years, I had another child while we lived there which was not part of my plan. I had already determined the marriage was not going to work within a few months.

My doctor advised me to stay off my feet with the pregnancy so I couldn't work. This meant I had to depend on my husband for everything. I hated to ask him for anything since I was used to having my own. I was miserable being so far from family and it was more arduous for my son. My son loved his grandparents; they were his babysitters for his first four years. I worked retail hours and stayed home with him on my days off or when I got off early. I was in retail management at a clothing store and often opened or closed the store. My parents had the chance to experience everything with my son before I did, such as taking his first steps.

My son and I made the best of our situation and he grew closer to me since I was the only one he had. I made a few friends while we lived there but I didn't like the D.C. area at all. I was a southern girl and the fast pace was too much for me. My husband was not an affectionate person, I realized that when we first moved there. One day he came home from work and I greeted him at the door. He walked away so I asked him what was wrong. He stated these words, "Nothing, this is the real me." I realized right then I had made a major mistake. He had only pretended to be nice, loving, and kind.

I was hundreds of miles from my home and completely isolated. All I thought was "Oh my God, what have I done!" He was mean and cruel for no reason at all and he controlled everything. He pushed the shopping cart, selected the food at the grocery store, and picked the accessories/furniture for the house. I tagged along like a voiceless object. I asked myself what kind of woman would stay with a man like that? The young woman that had walked out of one marriage and promised to do whatever it took to make this marriage work. We discussed staying together until the baby was born then we would go our separate ways. Yes, I gave up again because I just couldn't do it. After the birth of his son, my husband's behavior got better and we managed to exist for the sake of his son, his first child. Some months later he talked me into moving to Georgia when he received orders to transfer.

We moved from Washington, D.C. to Smyrna, Georgia. The first year was okay because I made new friends and enjoyed the area. Some Friday nights I had a chance to hang with my coworkers during the summer months. I enjoyed those outings so much and often looked forward to the gatherings. Then someone said, "Max let have the next one at your house since you haven't hosted before." I made up some excuse, but no one accepted my reason. Anxiety hit because I knew that was not a good idea. When time came around for me to host our girl's night I mentioned it to my husband. He didn't say anything about it. Why should he? He hung out with his friends and I never said anything. My children and I enjoyed that time together.

My friends came over and we did our usual stuff like playing cards, listening to music and talking about men, relationships, and the job. I never went into details with them about my husband; I would only say he was crazy and controlling. He left the house before they arrived and returned around 9:30 p.m. He walked in and my friends all spoke to him and he spoke and went straight to the bedroom. Quietness filled the room as the laughter and chatter stopped. The hand on the clock hit 10 p.m. and my husband walked out of the bedroom and said these exact words, "Maxine, it's time for you to go to bed, so your friends need to leave." He then turned around and went back into the bedroom. My friends looked at me, and without hesitation they quickly gathered the items they brought with them. As they left out the door they said, "Girl we will see you later, he's crazy." Of course they teased me forever about that, but they never asked me to host another gathering. Now they had witnessed his controlling behavior and craziness.

Sometimes your best is not good enough, we must know when to yield and when to allow God to fix what we messed up.

I told myself I had to try harder to make this marriage work and I couldn't just walk away without giving 100 percent. My first marriage was completely opposite. I was the head of the house and paid most of the bills because I made more money. We lived in an upscale apartment complex but he couldn't let go of his standing on the corner friends in his old neighborhood. He worked the second shift and before he went to work he hung out on the corner with them. Once he started drinking he didn't stop until he was drunk which meant he didn't go to work. He got fired from his job because he couldn't let go of his neighborhood friends on the corner. I knew I shouldn't have married him but my parents insisted since I was pregnant at the age of 21. I was a senior at Tennessee State University in Nashville, Tennessee and had to leave school. I knew in my heart he wouldn't be a good provider or father, and I told my parents I didn't want to get married just because I was pregnant. He was my high school boyfriend and he didn't go to college. Mom said these words to me, "You made your bed now lie in it and give that child a name." There was nothing else to discuss after her statement and one mistake became two mistakes. I finally got tired of paying all the bills, fighting, and looking in his intoxicated face. I was indeed my mother's daughter when it came to fighting. When I was in middle school I was always in trouble at school for fighting. I was not a bully and didn't start anything, but if someone stepped to me I always threw the first blow. The fighting stopped when I reached the 9th grade. I finally developed into a little lady and became a member of the Church of Christ. I tried my very best not to demonstrate that callous demeanor in my second marriage. I kept my hands to myself... well maybe I slipped a couple of times.

By the time my second husband and I reached our second year in Georgia he became worse than before. With two sons, the decision to leave was more difficult. I felt like a failure; two marriages, and two kids while still in my twenties. I vowed not to be like my mother but turned out to be my mother's daughter indeed. As a child I wanted my mother to take my brothers and me away from our dad so badly. I wanted to be away from all the violence but she never did. I finally got the confidence to leave my second husband and didn't care what anyone would think about me or say.

The mental and emotional abuse was more than I could continue to handle. I got home from work and found the house packed once again. That Friday morning everything was in order with no signs to show we were moving. I knew better than to ask why because his response would be the same, "You can go or you can stay." I was just glad it was during the summer this time, and I didn't have to transfer my oldest son again during the school year. I had saved all my money since I didn't have to pay household bills. I only paid for childcare since I wanted to work. I saved every penny because I knew it was a matter of time before I made a move. I refused to be like my mother since my tolerance for continued foolishness was low. My husband just didn't know the motive behind my eyes. Also, I decided to sleep in the bed with my oldest son that night; I could no longer pretend I was okay with his decision to move without telling me.

My husband came into the room and picked me up and laid me down on our bed. He was 6'5" and too strong for me to stop him as he forced himself upon me. I chose not to make a scene due to my children. That was his first time and surely his last time; my mind was set for leaving. The next morning my husband went to work since he was scheduled to work over the weekend which was a perfect time to get away. I had not quite planned out where I was going, but after that episode I was more determined to leave. Enough! I just wanted out and the only way I was going to take his son was to leave while he was at work. I gathered some items the next day after he left home and placed them in the car. I continued to gather things as I looked out the window. I saw his car approaching and didn't have time to get the other things. I grabbed the eight year old by the arm with my right hand and placed the three year old on my left hip. I ran and placed my sons in my car as he got out of his car. He saw the terror in my eyes as I drove away.

It was a high speed chase but determination ruled my foot while it was on the pedal, so I lost him in traffic. I drove around for an hour to make sure I had lost him. I was getting tired, it was early evening and my sons needed to eat. I don't remember what I fed them but I'm sure it was fast food. Now I was faced with finding a place to live and a place to stay for the night. I knew I wanted to be close to my job so I went to an apartment complex in proximity to my workplace. I went into the management office with my sons and explained to the leasing agent I needed an apartment. She told me that I needed to complete an application. I told her I needed an apartment now, today. The tears flowed as I told her I was running from my abusive husband. Also, I informed her I worked in the area and had money to pay for the apartment. She went into the office and came back with a set of keys to an apartment without me completing an application. She told me I could stay the night in the apartment and I gave her my ID to hold until I returned the next day.

The Most High God took control of the car and took us exactly where we needed to be. God had His angel waiting to help us. I knew my sons and I would be okay as we slept on the floor. I was freed from the mental and emotional abuse.

Inspirational Thoughts

If I could've talked to that younger me
I would have kept her from pain, sorrow and shame.
I would have shown her how to praise His holy name
To keep sane.
I would have told her of the many gifts inside
Before she believed lies.
I would have taught her how to love herself
To birth her worth
To diminish her hurt.
I would've looked into her eyes
Told her the truth
Held her hand to guide her through.
I wish she could have known what I know now
The difference between fake and real.

Nehemiah 8:10

*"Do not grieve, for the joy
of the Lord is your strength."*

Maxine Williams Wright

CHAPTER 2

God Changed It Around

WILLIE ARNEZ LA'MONTA BOOKER
Webb, Mississippi

As we go through life we have struggles, some spiritual and some we bring upon ourselves. Battles are raging all around us. I had to reflect back to the word of God many times in my life. The year 2018 was difficult but I was determined to have a stronger relationship with God. When I started to fast and pray it seemed as if the odds were against me.

On December 7, 2018 I was in a bad car accident while at work. I hydroplaned and woke up at Regional One Medical Center in the ICU. I tried to move my right arm and realized I could not make my arm move. I made every effort to move my arm but it was useless. Shortly after my efforts the doctor entered and informed me I would never be able to move my arm again. I became numb because my mind could not comprehend the remarks the doctor had just stated at that point. As the doctor continued to speak he also stated I needed to have surgery immediately. Not only was my right arm inoperable, I had broken vertebrae in my neck. The doctor's words slurred as I drifted into an unconscious state.

While in the hospital bed I asked myself how this could be. I was only 31 with a promising career in law enforcement. I was used to being active and now I felt hopeless for the first time in my life. My faith had always kept me and I knew God was not going to leave me now. Then I realized He was not through with me yet because He had more work for me to do. God brought me through the surgery successfully. I knew He orchestrated every aspect of the surgery and now I had to wait for the process of His healing.

After being released from the hospital I started the physical therapy. The therapy sessions lasted a period of eight months which seemed endless. I had the support of my wife and other family members which provided nourishment to my emotional and mental state of being. I went before God as His humble servant for I knew all things were in His divine will. I studied the word of God more to develop a closer relationship with Him. As I prayed and studied my fragile body became stronger and more agile.

Through the healing process I had to deal with my financial situation since the bills did not stop. Being the protector, provider and leader of my family I was also concerned how I would maintain myself spiritually and mentally. I endured many sleepless nights from stress and the discomfort my body was experiencing. That's when I was reminded that "All things work together for the good to them that love God, to them who are called according to His purpose." (Romans 8:28) That's right, I was made on purpose for His purpose. God continued to show himself stronger and mightier, mightier and stronger in my life.

The voice of God will soothe your spirit.

God spoke plain as day in my spirit that He would keep me in perfect peace if I kept my mind focused on Him. When I changed my mindset and relinquished the negativity I began to see profitable situations before my very eyes. I unintentionally placed limitations on God, but within my heart I knew He would supply all my needs. No matter what we are faced with in life Jesus is waiting to bring us out victoriously if we submit to Him wholeheartedly.

Maxine Williams Wright

I am grateful to be under the leadership of Bishop Calvin C. Wiley and LaDonna A. Wiley of the City of Refuge Church in Batesville, Mississippi. They encouraged me and spoke life over me. It's vital that we are under true leadership and that our leaders are concerned about our relationship with God. It is God's will that we shall live and not die. "The thief cometh not, but for to steal, and to kill, and to destroy: I am come that they might have life, and that they might have it more abundantly." (John 10:10)

The doctor told me I was not going to have usage in my right arm, but the doctor didn't know the God I served. God changed it around for the better. I went from being motionless in my right arm to being able to complete Mississippi Conservation Officer Training Academy as a Mississippi Game Warden. No matter how hard life gets, no matter how the devil tries to discourage you continue to trust in GOD.

*God **showered** me with blessings on top of **blessings!***

Testimonies

God's Unfolding Miracles

Inspirational Thoughts

How many times have you reflected back on the struggles and inconceivable situations you found yourself in? You try to develop a stronger relation to let God know you need Him. But instead of things getting better they get worse and you find yourself in a detrimental state. It may seem like you're comatose without resolution. Just when you thought your relationship with God had become stronger, a life and death occurrence happens. You question your walk with Him and try to determine what caused you to be in this critical moment. The cliché "Here today and gone tomorrow" comes to mind, or should it be "Here this moment and gone the next moment." No matter what you are faced with you must know all things are for your good.

God will put you in a situation for you to completely depend on Him. You say you believe and have faith. But do you really? The mouth and the heart speak differently sometimes, just like your words and your actions are often not in sync. Will your faith rely on the hands of the surgeons or will you rely on God's hands to guide the hands of the surgeons? By choosing God's hands the situation will become more beneficial. Not only do you rely on God to heal you, you must rely on Him to orchestrate your life. When you surrender to His will and allow God to take control, all things work together for you and to glorify The Most High God.

The witness sharing his story was reminded that all things work together for the good to them that love God. The witness feared not for he knew the power of The Most High God.

Isaiah 41:10

*"So do not fear, for I am with you; do not be dismayed, for
I am your God. I will strengthen you and help you; I will
uphold you with my righteous right hand."*

Maxine Williams Wright

CHAPTER 3

A Miracle in the Hospital

WANDA J. BOOKER-WADE
Memphis, Tennessee

My school years at Humes Jr. High School were an exciting time for me. Back then we called it Junior High instead of Middle School and the grades were 7th, 8th, and 9th. I was active in the school band and played the clarinet for the entire three years at Humes. I'm not sure why I selected the clarinet from all the other instruments but I liked the distinct sound it made. I enjoyed the atmosphere of the band where we were all unique musicians with one sound as we moved to the same rhythm. Our band teacher/director was phenomenal. He taught us what it meant being in a band. It was the highlight of my day when I was in band class and band rehearsal. I was in a state of amazement when we performed at school and in parades. During the 8th grade, I was nominated and won Miss Band. I was so thankful I received those accolades from my peers.

Let me take you back to my first year at Humes which was a difficult time for me and my family. In 1976 I was only 11 years old in the 7th grade and I was the oldest of five. I took on some of the responsibilities with my younger siblings since my mom worked fulltime and needed help, but she did allow me to continue with school activities. During those days neighbors would watch out when our parents were not home. So you better be on your best behavior because the neighbors would surely tell. One day I noticed a medium sized soft knot on the right side of my neck. It had appeared overnight because I didn't recall it being there the day before. It wasn't sore to touch, just uncomfortable and it felt weird. Being young I didn't understand the severity of the knot but I had enough sense to know I needed to tell my mother. So I mentioned the knot to mom and she decided to watch it to see if it was going to get bigger. Sure enough it got bigger overnight. The size of the knot hindered my speech and I could only speak in a whisper the next morning which caused great concerns. My sisters and brother looked stunned because they didn't know what was wrong with me. At that time I didn't know what was wrong with me either and I don't recall if there was any pain, just discomfort.

God hears our faintest cry, just a little talk with Jesus makes it right.

My mother called off from work and took me to Le Bonheur Children's Hospital. The hospital was close to our neighborhood so we walked. Mom didn't know how to drive at that time so we didn't have a car. Everything was convenient in our neighborhood so most people didn't have cars. And if you needed to go out of the neighborhood you caught the bus. Her job was within three miles from home and her mother, dad, and aunt were less than a mile away. It only took us 20 minutes to get to the hospital. I was checked into the emergency room where they conducted x-rays and plenty of tests. After the examinations I was immediately admitted. The doctors didn't know what to make of the knot on my neck so they gave me IV fluids. During the course of my one week stay in the hospital my mother checked on me early in the mornings before she went to work. I knew it was demanding on mom because she walked to see me and then she walked further up the street to go to work every day. There were four other children in the household so her hands were full. One morning mom came to visit and I needed help to the restroom. I noticed something different when I stood. The bottom of my feet felt like I was walking on rocks which were very uncomfortable, but I endured the pain and didn't give up.

The school assigned a tutor while I was hospitalized in order for me not to fall behind in my classes. What I missed most about school was attending my classes, playing my clarinet, and the fellowship I had with the other band members. The doctors informed my mother that they contacted specialists at St. Jude. The doctors planned to come together to determine the prognosis. As I listened to them discuss the circumstances with mom, I saw a different expression come upon her face. Everyone in Memphis knew St. Jude doctors dealt with cancer patients which brought tears to my mother's eyes. I didn't know what was going on and didn't fully understand the possible outcome. The St. Jude doctors and the Le Bonheur doctors did an assessment on my neck and determined there was definitely an amount of fluid that needed to be drained. The doctors determined they needed to lance the knot either the next day or within a couple of days. They explained the process to my mother and she informed her mother. Then my grandmother told other family members what the doctors planned to do. I know now that prayers were sent before God on my behalf, and I'm so thankful I had a praying mother and grandmother!

Glory be to God! The knot disappeared on my neck the day before they planned to perform the surgery and my feet no longer felt like I was walking on rocks. It was truly, truly a miracle because the doctors intended to operate on me. They thoroughly examined me but there was no soreness and the knot was gone. It was as if it had never happened! I didn't know anything about God, about prayer, but God was definitely looking out for me even when I didn't know it. Now I know at this stage of my life that my God had plans for me. The doctors later discover that I had a rare blood disorder called Thalassemia Anemia which was manageable. I was so happy to be able to return to school and continue my school activities with more appreciation for things we take for granted such as being able to walk without pain and being able to speak clearly. My classmates and teachers were so happy to see me and were supportive through that phase of my life.

All I can say is I am truly grateful to God for blessing me in such a miraculous way!! He didn't have to allow things to turn around for me, but He did. He is Jehovah-Rapha, the God who heals! He did it for me and He can do it for you!! Glory be to God!!

When I became an adult I was reassessed by a cancer doctor in Southaven, Mississippi. I still have this rare blood disorder that will be with me for the rest of my life. And my God also will be with me for the rest of my Life!

I'm so thankful
I had a **praying**
mother and grandmother!

Maxine Williams Wright

Inspirational Thoughts

Memorable experiences can happen when you're a youth that can cause life changing moments with ripple effects. When you're young the last thing on your mind is becoming ill. Most young people think they are forever young with a carefree, happy go lucky attitude. They are consumed with enjoyable and jubilant activities and their bandwidth is indescribable. So how can you receive accolades one moment and the next moment you receive disturbing news about your health? Your mind doesn't grasp what your body is going through.

Your heart bounces with sporadic, uncertain rhythms moving to unrecognizable voices in your head. You realize you don't have a close connection with God and the sounds are muffled. You really don't know what to do or what to think or whom to turn. When you think all is hopeless, He will give you back your tomorrow and make it even better than today. He's a God of second chances.

The witness was too young to realize God had a relationship with her. He knew her before she knew herself. He will place others around to give you what you need, to help you hear His voice. Through the muffled sounds His voice will rule, His commands obeyed and His will be done. The Most High God has already outlined your path. He knows the work you must do to glorify His kingdom, to guide others in need of light, to speak life into dying souls, to awaken deaf ears, and to mend broken relationships. Listen, do you hear Him?

Exodus 15:2

"The Lord is my strength and my song; he has given me victory. This is my God, and I will praise him— my father's God, and I will exalt him."

Maxine Williams Wright

CHAPTER 4

But God Blessed Him

ERNEST L. FOSTER
Powder Springs, Georgia

He had it all! Youth, brains, education, success and a beautiful fiancée. He was a Lieutenant Colonel in the United States Air Force and had never expected to marry again, but God blessed him. In 1990 at age 40, he married the most beautiful lady in the world. He was intelligent and successful; she was intelligent, successful, and beautiful! They both were high achievers with wonderful, good paying jobs. Their future looked bright! They were destined to live on top of the world. Or was their union cursed?

His wife's previous husband had died two years earlier of lung cancer. The colonel looked liked the epitome of health. He had never experienced a serious health challenge in his life. But less than a year after his marriage, the colonel was diagnosed with coronary heart disease. Of the three main arteries supplying blood to his heart, two were 100% blocked and the third artery was 45% blocked. After he heard the diagnoses provided by the doctor and listened to the doctor's description of his problems, he felt hopeless. Satan whispered in the colonel's ear that he would be dead within two or three years. The bible says that the devil is a liar, yet the colonel believed this liar. But God blessed him.

His doctor presented his case to the cardiology department of 16 doctors. Several of the doctors felt that an immediate by-pass operation was in order. However, as a department they decided to treat his condition with medications. The doctors stated this was only a temporary solution and sooner or later a by-pass operation would be required.

A year later, in 1992 the colonel was diagnosed with diabetes. He was required to take more than one pill each day to treat the diabetes in addition to his coronary heart disease diagnosis. Over the years his diabetes worsened. By 2001 in addition to the pills, he was now taking insulin several times per day. Satan had him convinced that he would never live to see his son grow up to finish college, get married, have kids, and have a successful career. The colonel was convinced that he would be dead soon. He had even discussed his medical situation with his son to prepare him for the inevitable. He made arrangements with his sister to take care of his son if he was to die. Oh yes, the Evil One had him convinced that death for him was just around the corner. But God blessed him.

By 2002 his coronary heart disease had also worsened to the point that he was scheduled for a triple by-pass operation. During the procedure, the doctors found a 4th clogged artery, so he ended up with a quadruple by-pass operation. Since his original diagnosis he had often pondered on how wonderful it would be if he could just live to reach age 60. He wanted to witness his son succeed in life but he never believed it would happen. But God blessed him.

By His stripes we are healed.

Yes, God blessed him real good. Today, some 30 years since his original diagnosis:

- He is still living!
- He is still married to his beautiful bride.
- He has not taken insulin in over 13 years.
- He plays golf about twice per week.
- He celebrated his 70th birthday in 2020.
- All things considered, his health is quite good.

Yes, God blessed him real good. He lived to see his son:

- Graduate from high school.
- Go to college and become an aerospace engineer.
- Get married to a wonderful wife (May 2000).
- Receive his Master's degree and many other accolades throughout the years.
- Retire as a major from the United States Air Force.
- Set an example for his two boys on how to be a wonderful husband and father.

You may be wondering how I know so many details about this colonel's life. Well, the details are about my own life. You see, I am the colonel and God has truly blessed me over and over and over again!

ERNEST L. FOSTER, Lt Colonel, USAF (Ret)
THIS IS MY STORY AND I'M STICKING TO IT!!!

*God **blessed** me*
***real** good!*

Testimonies
God's Unfolding Miracles

Maxine Williams Wright

Inspirational Thoughts

It feels great feeling like you are on top of the world. Life has been good to you. You feel God's favor and blessings upon your life and you are grateful. You have experienced some misfortunes but for the most part everyone has at one time or another. You can count it all joy when you fall and get up knowing The Most High God is there to catch you when you stumble.

No matter what you see or what you are told, without a doubt you believe that all things are possible with God. Your outcome will be victorious when God is by your side. You put forth your best efforts to withstand as your legs become weak. But within an instant you regain power and confidence for you know God will not forsake you. You refuse to become a victim to lies of the enemy.

You stand on God's word yet your prayers are unanswered. So what do you do when all hope is gone? You stand! You believe! You praise! You glorify Him… whatever the outcome! He blessed the witness many times. The witness went through many health issues and despite his medical challenges, the witness believed. Instead of feeling hopeless, feel hopeful. Instead of listening to negative thoughts, tune to positive vibrations.

When God has a mission for your life you are often a target. The negative forces don't want you to serve, to heal, to lead, and to nourish. God has a purpose for you!

Joshua 1:9

"Be strong and courageous; do not be frightened and do not be dismayed, for the Lord your God is with you wherever you go."

Maxine Williams Wright

CHAPTER 5

Life vs. Death

MARVIN BALDWIN, JR.
Atlanta, Georgia

The thing about life is that no one can tell you how your life is going to pan out. Growing up in St. Louis, Missouri as a mischievous child I constantly got into trouble in the Pine Lawn neighborhood. I was indeed a problem adolescent; I've cheated, I've stolen, I've inflicted pain, I've caused emotional distress, I've lied, and I've destroyed lives. I can recall the day my path to crime was laid out. My family and I lived in the projects, I was only eight years old when my stepfather, who is now deceased, showed me a knife. At the time I wasn't quite sure why he showed me his knife. I soon learned as he spoke the words that would change my very essence. "This is how you get away with murder. You stick a person and throw the weapon in the river." Out of all the things he taught and showed me, that stood out the most. I'm sure he thought he was teaching me something of value. I still don't understand to this day why he said that to me. A person can only teach what they know. In fact, that lesson carried with me throughout my life of crime.

I grew up in a home where there was domestic violence. I didn't realize how impactful growing up in a toxic environment could be on a person. I'm reminded of this verse in Proverbs 22:6, "Train up a child in the way they should go and when they get old he will not depart from it." I can honestly say that was most definitely true in my case. That seed was planted and took root in my soul, the seed of deception, rage, and defiance. This is the reason we must be involved with our children and establish a form of communication while they are young. Everyone cannot pour into your child. My stepfather poured death into me on that day, but he thought he was teaching me to live and to survive.

I grew up surrounded by violence. My environment consumed me and I became angry and violent. I was a young man who projected my anger onto others and dared anyone to cross me. I was indeed a force to be reckoned with. That one incident in particular I remember quite vividly. I was sitting on the front porch with a friend while he visited his girl one summer evening. Out of nowhere a few gang members pulled up from another set. They had one of the girls who lived in my neighborhood in the car. The guys saw us on the porch and proceeded to drive off because we were at my friend's girlfriend house. The young lady from my neighborhood yelled out from the car, "That ain't nobody but Lil Budd." So the driver puts the car in reverse because my friend had a reputation. I told my friend, "As soon as they step foot out that car, I'm dumping on them." I pulled my 38 revolver out of my pants and sat it on my lap. The guy in the rear passenger seat opened the door and as soon as his foot hit the ground I shot the car up. They tried to pull off but I must have hit the motor. I shot the windows out for sure, but I don't know to this day if I shot someone. My friend and I didn't stick around to find out. This is an example of my path of death.

Jesus will be your beacon of light in the midst of darkness.

The end of the road was exactly the end of life for me. There were no detours, no yield signs, and no caution lights. My spirit begged for life while at the end of the road. The smell and taste of death had consumed me. I couldn't take it anymore, I felt defeated and surrendered to the voice within. I knew there was an option for me, I just needed to be in the house of God to find a needed change. I had a nickel plated 25 automatic, a wad of dope, and a roll of money in my pocket when I entered through the doors. I felt redemption when I entered the haven for defeated souls. I sat on the back row and that was the beginning of my new life. I remember that day like today.

After that day my life was never the same. I chose life, I chose another path, and I chose a meaningful existence. Because of the decision to choose the path of life I discovered my purpose, my gifts, and my inner peace. I became an Actor, Published Author, Motivational Speaker, Screenwriter, Radio Personality, Investor, etc. Everything I choose today is to raise my vibrations and to cause others to become the best version of self.

Marvin "MBJ Live" Baldwin, Jr.
mindbodysoulhealer@yahoo.com
IG: @therealmindbodysoulhealer
FB: MBJ Live
TW: @MarvinBaldwinJr

I ***chose*** *to*
raise my ***vibrations!***

Inspirational Thoughts

There are circumstances you don't have any control of when you enter this world such as your parents, your demographics, your family, and your financial status. You play the hand you were given the best you can. You hold your ace in your pocket and will use it when needed. You are a product of your environment. You have no value for life with a ruthless reputation. You exist without knowing your worth. Do you know anyone sleeping on their talents? I call them sleep gifters? I was also a sleep gifter.

The witness made a decision to change. He had reached his end of the road. He listened to the voice he heard which was the voice of The Most High God. The witness had to surrender to God's voice if he wanted life. The life of the witness had not been easy; he only played the game he was exposed to. Instead of him rising above his environment he became a victim. He chose to survive the best way he knew how. So many get caught up and don't find a way out of these situations. Can you imagine the many talents in the grave, in jail, and on drugs? The witness escaped those options when he obeyed God's voice. He chose life and discovered his gifts. When The Most High God has a mission for you, He will snatch you from the depths of your pit. He will replace your pain with gain.

Think about it this way. You're at the plate and you strikeout. How would you feel if you strikeout in every game? Eventually your team would lose faith in you and you would lose faith in yourself. Now imagine yourself at the plate and Jesus throws the ball, He wants you to hit a home run. You still strikeout but He continues to throw the ball to you and gives you more than three tries. He won't give up on you, He knows your ability, He knows you need more time, and He knows you can make the right swing. And just like that you hit the ball and it's a home run. Even if you strikeout, keep trying, keep showing up, keep aiming, and keep swinging.

Isaiah 12:2

"Surely God is my salvation; I will trust and not be afraid. The Lord, the Lord, is my strength and my song; he has become my salvation."

Maxine Williams Wright

CHAPTER 6

The Dream

ANDREW BOOKER (OOW WEE MAN)
Tutwiler, Mississippi

I learned my strengths and weaknesses at an early age. School was a major challenge because no matter how hard I studied I found it difficult. I finally realized that God gave us all different gifts which I understood, acknowledged, and accepted. I felt music deep in my bones and I knew that was my God given gift. When He gives you something no one but God can take it away from you. So I accepted my challenges while in school and did the best I could do… only by the grace of God.

In the scriptures God used all types of people. God looks within to find the depth of your essence to use for His glory. The just and unjust received blessings from the sun and the rain. Each day that I witnessed the rising of the sun I considered to be a blessed day. No longer did I focus on what I didn't have or couldn't do. Instead I was grateful for what I did have and what I could do. I knew with God all things were possible. I was indeed God's child despite my inabilities.

When I discovered my gift of music at a young age I was consumed with the style of the Blues. I listened to B.B. King, Muddy Waters, and many other blues singers. Within my heart I knew I wanted to be a Blues singer. Music came easy to me and no matter how good I was my father did not approve. My mother, on the other hand, encouraged me to play and to sing blues songs while I was a child. Whenever my father was not home mom and I took advantage of that time. Mom would say, "Go get your guitar and play some Muddy Waters." I would play and my mother would sing. Those were the best of times I shared with my mother. It was good to see her have a good time as we enjoyed ourselves but kept watch for my father. We made sure we were playing and singing gospel songs when we saw him from a distance through the window.

Through the years I continued to play the blues without my father's knowledge. It was best to keep peace in the house and I surely didn't want to get mom involved. When I became an adult I didn't need to hide or get his approval. I played and sang secular music with many different bands. In 2010 I went solo and produced my first CD in 2011 titled "I Miss My Mom 'N' Dad." The dream I had as a child had come true and I was a Blues singer.

As a young man I was foolish and I knew it was the grace of God that kept me while on this journey. When I thought about where I came from and where I am today, I knew God had kept His hands on me! When I thought I wasn't smart enough, God assured me I didn't have to be like anyone else. We all have a mold and no one else will ever be able to fit the mold God designed just for you.

Embrace who you are and don't compare yourself to anyone. You are good enough! From picking cotton at the age of 12 and making $6 dollars a day to blessings others with the gifts God gave me. "It was He who gave some to be apostles, some to be prophets, some to be evangelists, and some to be pastors and teachers, to prepare God's people for works of service, so that the body of Christ may be built up until we all reach unity in the faith and in the knowledge of the Son of God and become mature, attaining to the whole measure of the fullness of Christ." (Ephesians 4:11-13)

God gave us all some and I am good enough!

Inspirational Thoughts

You often don't understand when you put forth your best and still can't succeed, you can lose hope. The mold God designed for you is only for you, and the mold He designed for someone else is only for someone else. There's nothing wrong putting forth your best. For example, I've always liked dancing. I used to practice in the mirror but couldn't move to the rhythm of the music. When I tried to spin I got dizzy, and let's just say, I would never be a dancer. Just because you lack in one specific area doesn't mean you don't have a gift. When you discover your gift you're appreciative and grateful. Your gift has always been there undiscovered. Sometimes someone else can see something special in you that you cannot see in yourself. It's easy to compare yourself to others and conclude that they are better. But with any gift it takes time for development. You must put in time, you must stay focused, you must make a commitment, and you must be grateful to God for your gift.

When the witness stopped comparing himself to others he discovered his own gift. Everyone is not Albert Einstein. I had the same problem comparing myself to others. I focused on what I couldn't do. It took many years to unlock the chains that had me bound. You can be your worst critic. Once you let go of the negative thoughts you will be able to develop your gifts. Get out of your own way. Like the witness said, "God gave us all some!" Some might have more than others and that is alright. No matter what age you are, it's never too late to use your gifts. Be grateful and know where your gifts come from.

Your mold is intentional for your purpose.

Isaiah 40:29

*"He gives power to the weak
and strength to the powerless."*

Maxine Williams Wright

CHAPTER 7

In the Palm of His Hand

PAULA G VOICE
Marietta, Georgia

My marriage is over! After 23 years, it is over! The rug is pulled out from under you! You get a good punch to the stomach that knocks the wind out of you! We each may have experienced that sensation at some point in our lives. This was one of those moments for me. Devastated, depressed, lost, confused, angry... I could keep going. However, I think you probably get the idea! I was a hot mess! Life would never be the same and I had no idea what it would look like. I began the painful and long journey of trying to put my life back together. You see, my mind had been set on "till death do us part." At the time I knew of no other life but that of being a military spouse and the duties and responsibilities that came along with that. I was married a year or so after graduating from college. Not long after that we received orders to relocate to Germany which was where I lived for the next three years. That was the routine for the next 20 years of military assignments, living on military installations, and the life of an army wife. That was it! What was I to do now that my marriage had ended? Where would I go? How would I live? How would my daughters handle this? I had a bachelor's degree but hadn't really worked in my field since I was moving every three years or so. Jobs came based on where we were stationed. Home was where the army sent you and there were not always job opportunities waiting for your arrival as a military spouse.

Living overseas was quite challenging for employment. Returning home was a challenge as well due to few employers not willing to hire a military spouse because they knew she would be gone in three years or so. Jobs came but they were generally temporary for only a few years. Single and civilian, I found myself facing graduate school at the age of 45! The first day I walked into class I felt some kind of way. "OMG! I am the oldest one in here!" These folks could be my children! Talk about feeling self-conscious! Can someone tell me what a flash drive is? Power who? Power point? Is that like Wonder Woman when she points? "Wonder power!" Is that a PowerPoint? Do you all see my dilemma!?! God has a way of placing who and what you need in the right place at the right time. I found myself with a great cohort and we were a great balance. Everyone brought a needed strength to the table that allowed us to work together and have a successful graduate school experience. The younger generation compiled the technological aspects, I compiled the content and we presented our projects. It worked! A great friendship developed among us. This great friendship and balance were truly evident when my car accident occurred.

On November 10, 2004 I was on my way to Borders (bookstore that was open at the time) to work on an assignment for my graduate class. Courtney (my youngest daughter) and her drums were normally with me that time of day. She had an afterschool practice, so she and her drums were still at school. This will be significant in a minute. I was about three blocks from the bookstore, at a stop light waiting for the light to change. I drove an older model Nissan Altima which was a relatively small to medium sized vehicle. Way in the distance I could see a vehicle approaching behind me but didn't pay much attention. I assumed that they would slow down and stop behind me. They were moving at a high rate of speed but who doesn't on that particular parkway. It has been known to be the site of late night drag racing by fearless teenagers. A few seconds later I looked up again and saw the grill of a Yukon SUV coming through the back window of my car. Remember I mentioned that Courtney and her tenor drums (quads) were usually with me in the car?

I remember being banged and spun around like I was in the bumper car ride at the carnival. When the car finally came to a stop, m head felt like it was trying to explode! The pain was indescribable and I was struggling for coherency. I couldn't move and was wondering where the water was coming from that was streaming down from the top of my head. I tried to wipe it away so I could see. My hands were completely red as I wiped the "water" away. I realized at that moment that I was bleeding profusely from my head (which was banging in excruciating pain). There was a lot of yelling and screaming from outside the car. Someone kept screaming, "Oh my God!" That scared me because I just knew one of my limbs must have been lying out on the pavement and that is why she was saying, "Oh my God!"

God sends angels during a crisis.

Someone took hold of my hand that was covered in blood. All I remember was him saying his name JT and that everything was going to be alright. I never saw or heard from that man again but I was so grateful for his calming effect. I honestly believe I would have gone into shock from the pain coming from my head. Also, the thought that I must have lost a limb caused fear because the "Oh my God" woman was on her 50th "Oh my God!" Firemen were on top of the car cutting away the roof. My seat belt was cut off by a paramedic. A flat board was placed behind me and my head was strapped in a stationary manner. Amidst the loud drill of the "jaws of life," the yelling, screaming and sirens, a paramedic and JT were doing their best to keep me calm. I was in unbearable pain. Panic and shock were setting in and more pain shot through my body as they were trying to remove me from the car. I felt like I was going in and out of consciousness.

It was a cold November day and I recall the paramedics having to cut my clothes off so they could determine if I was bleeding elsewhere or what other injuries were present. I'm shivering on a stretcher in the middle of the street in nothing but my underwear. All I could think of was what your mama used to tell you: "You better wear clean underwear in case you get in a car accident!" Why is Mama always right? My underwear was clean but my major concern at that moment was, "Am I matching? Did I put on a matching bra and panty set?!?!?!?" Don't judge me! Ladies, because you know you would be thinking the same thing! LOL! Now THAT is a true "Oh my God" moment! Fortunately I did. It's interesting the things you think of in crisis. I think that is your mind's way of survival. Distracting from the crisis at hand. I remember JT's voice; he was very irritated! He asked the paramedics, "Can't you cover her up?" Someone eventually covered me and I was placed into the ambulance. It was at that moment that my thoughts shifted from underwear to the realization that I did indeed have all my limbs. Then I got angry at that woman continuously screaming "Oh my God!" What was she screaming about!?!? I had all my limbs! The reason behind her screams was later revealed.

It was not until a few weeks that I learned that my car was the first of 11 vehicles hit by that same SUV. The police report indicated that the SUV hit the rear of my car at 85 mph. Insurance companies can be a bit insensitive at times. Since I was alone and in the midst of a divorce, I did not have my spouse to take care of certain things. Therefore, I had to find someone willing to take me to the junk yard to claim my car. Still broken, bandaged, dizzy and weak, I managed to get a ride to the junk yard. That was a long ride! Figuratively speaking as it was the first time I was in a car after the accident. Panic hit! Nausea and dizziness hit! Upon arrival, I visually searched for my vehicle as I couldn't walk extremely far at all. As I looked, I could see the expression on the person's face who gave me a ride to the junk yard. I was instructed to look to my right. As I did, I nearly collapsed. The entire back half of the vehicle was shattered. The roof was bent and caved in. The only part of the car that was somewhat intact was the driver's seat. The car was barely recognizable.

There is a saying that God places a hedge of protection around us. I associate a hedge with yard space since hedges usually surround the property line of a home. God did not place a hedge of protection around me. He held me in the palm of His hands. The only part of the car that was not severely crushed was the driver's seat where I was sitting. I always sat close to the steering wheel when I drove. The doctor said if my seat was further back, I would have been killed. I know without a doubt, God brought me through that near-death experience for a reason. This journey is part of that reason. I call that day my 2nd birthday. I vowed to spend each day with the breath I am given to speak life into others. To do what God has equipped me to do. To encourage you to do what God has equipped you to do. You see, God brings us through near death experiences or illnesses for a reason. He wants to show us that He always has us in the palm of His hand. We in turn must share the testimony so that others can experience the depths of His love, protection, and provision for us. No matter your circumstances and regardless how devastating, if you are living and breathing, that means God brought you through and has given you a testimony! Testify about His goodness! Testify about His love! Testify that with God, all things are indeed possible. Testify! Be encouraged! Embrace the journey!

"I am Paula G Voice! I am a sagacious, independent-lifestyle influencer. I am embracing my own journey and I am sharing a soliloquy of seasons on the journey. I am influencing dreamers to do the same by breathing life into their vision and ultimately living the reality of that vision! It is never too late to embrace your journey and live your dream! Visit Paula's Blog at www.paulagvoice.com for additional soliloquies of the journey."

A *hedge* of *protection* around me!

Inspirational Thoughts

Change is often uncomfortable and unfamiliar. Just when you think you're on target, life throws a dart and completely misses the mark of your bullseye. Your expectation is not always the same as your counterpart. You can go through your daily routines believing all is well until the fuse is ignited. It's like walking in a combat zone mine field only not knowing you're walking in a mine field. The explosion causes effects that will place you on the path to your destiny.

God will set you up without you knowing it. Sometimes He has to remove you from your current situation in order to get your full attention and to get to your potential. It's not about you but about the demands only you can mend, only you can provide, only you can attend. God will relocate you to get your full worth. When you depend on, rely on, focus on, and trust in someone besides Him you are depending on a person, and God wants you to depend on Him.

God will rearrange priorities for the glory of His kingdom. He will alter schedules, clear out back car seats, and surround you with His angels to protect you. No harm will come to you when you have purpose. You must complete your assignment. When you're chosen, you're special and you need to recognize the favor upon your life. Others may not understand the degree of your assignment and ask how and why. As long as God is on your side, that's all you need.

The witness developed a closer relationship with God. She didn't understand why she had to change her lifestyle. She didn't understand the new journey. When she discovered her purpose, she discovered her gifts, and she discovered her worth. And she knew it was His grace that saved her in the car accident. The witness got back on the battlefield to continue her mission.

When God has plans for you, nothing will be able to stop you. Sometimes you take detours, wrong turns, and run past caution lights. But when you develop a relationship with God, He will work on your behalf. He will place His full armor around you.

Ain't no mountain high enough, ain't no valley low enough, and ain't no river wide enough to keep you from your purpose.

God is Good!

1 Peter 5:10

"And the God of all grace, who called you to his eternal glory in Christ, after you have suffered a little while, will himself restore you and make you strong, firm and steadfast."

Maxine Williams Wright

CHAPTER 8

Abiding In My Father's House

Rev. Teronda P. Hamilton
Powder Springs, Georgia

It was late September. My two best friends had decided as new Christians, this would be the year we would go to the Church of God in Christ (C.O.G.I.C.) Annual Convocation in Washington, D.C. I had a plan to make it work. After asking, we would stay at my dad's house 50 miles away. This narrative meant no lodging cost, renting a car to get to the convocation, staying all day, eating snacks, then returning to my dad's house. The total expenses for the car rental and gas would be split between us. A great trip was in store with plenty of time to save and prepare by November. We purchased our non-refundable plane tickets right then to ensure we were not going to change our minds. None of us would waste money like that.

Then everything that could happen unexpectedly occurred to keep me from saving. The greatest expense was the propane tank used to heat the house, for hot water and cooking became empty. I knew nothing about how to read the gauge on the tank. My husband was on one of his disappearing acts (another story) so I was on my own. I called the company to come out for a refill. They left an extremely large bill which wiped out my funds. Unbeknownst to me, the tank became empty again within a week. I questioned if they really filled it, I did not know. I just knew we couldn't function with an empty propane tank. I managed to get it refilled with the help of a family friend who also made sure it was full. By now it was October and my resources were completely depleted due to the necessity to refill the tank. The trip was in a couple of weeks and decisions had to be made.

How could I cover my share of the expenses? I needed every penny to take care of my children so I couldn't go. Yet, how could I do that to my friends? If I didn't go, they couldn't. They couldn't cover the trip expenses without my contributing portion. We arranged the trip according to our resources so I couldn't expect them to absorb my percentage. Also, there was the matter of the non-refundable plane tickets already purchased. I just couldn't expect them to handle all the expenses so I simply had no choice but to go. While my excitement had diminished, I just knew I couldn't cancel on them. This decision had nothing to do with faith. I had not yet learned that since it was early in my Christian walk. So as the day of departure arrived, I hid my burden as we boarded the plane. All the while in my heart I was praying to God, "What am I going to do?"

As we made our descent into the Washington Dulles International Airport, I felt sick to my stomach and felt weak. We walked through the terminal, gathered our luggage, and then I saw my dad's face. The sight of his smile made the trip worthwhile. He extended his outstretched arms and I collapsed into them as a wail of tears fell. Turning from my friends, I couldn't stop the emotional turmoil soaring throughout my body.

Dad pulled me to the side with a very puzzled look and asked, "Ronnie, what's wrong?" I told him, "I shouldn't have come. I have no money for my share of the expenses, I'm just here and don't know what to do." With a stronger embrace he whispered, "Promise you will never ever not come to me just because you lack the funds. I will take care of everything. Money should never be a concern between us. Promise me if you need anything for yourself, my grandchildren or any other necessity, just ask."

I was at ease knowing that my dad never broke a promise to me, so my trip was off to a brighter start. My friends and I traveled to the convocation in D.C. daily without having to rent a car. How? My dad allowed us to use his car with a full tank of gas. Before we left at 7:30 a.m. he told us dinner would be ready when we returned. That was another expense we eliminated. Dad had prepared a dinner fit for queens. We had steaks with baked potatoes, asparagus, dinner rolls, pasta with meat sauce, garlic bread, and salad. Every night was something new, special, unexpected, and extravagant. One evening my brother came over and popped some microwave popcorn. Dad overheard my friend say that she wished she had some popcorn. The next morning on top of the microwave, what did we see? A box of microwave popcorn was waiting just for us, without having to ask. The kitchen was filled with a variety of fruits and snacks.

You shall not be deprived in your Father's house.

The convocation in D.C. had great speakers and workshops, yet unrelated to my greatest lessons and experiences. In spite of that it was still a great week in the presence of God, quality time with dad, and the fellowship with my friends. My father made the week great by extending the purest unconditional love to me and my friends. Though he had never met my friends he made sure they felt welcomed. At the close of a long day we were blessed beyond our expectations.

After many nightly conversations with my dad about situations at home, dad made an offer on our last night. He offered to eliminate the burdens I faced at home. He said, "Go home, quit your job, pack up your things and move here. I'll take care of you. Go home and think about it." Dad could do it as a retiree with a military pension, retiree from the National Institute of Health as a bio-chemist with a pension, and with his social security. I didn't doubt his words, but could I do that?

As I boarded the plane and took my seat away from the others, I began to reflect on all my years with my dad. Annual plane rides from Kansas City, Kansas to Frederick, Maryland starting at age four every summer. I spent summers with dad from the day after the last day of school until the day before school was to begin again until age seventeen. Those summers were filled with educational adventures that fed my love of history. There were no historical sites unseen in Washington, D.C. I saw the Smithsonian Museums, the Arlington Cemetery with the changing of the guards, the memorial John F. Kennedy Eternal Flame, and the Battlefields of Gettysburg.

I wanted to see New York so Dad orchestrated a tour bus full to take me. We went to Hershey Park, home of the chocolate candy bar and so much more. While in Frederick I found other historical sites such as The Francis Scott Key Monument and the home of Betsy Ross. And in our own backyard dad made cutting grass a time of fun with my two younger sisters and three brothers. We even enjoyed rides under the shady trees in the graveyard adjacent to our home. Yes, even that was an adventure. Dad taught me to swim at the park where he worked as a part-time lifeguard. While summers with dad were great, he never forgot me upon returning home for school. He always took care of me, sending surprise boxes of toys and clothes. His presence was always known whether seen or unseen. There couldn't have been a greater dad in the entire world in my eyes, even to this day. I was always teary-eyed when I had to return to Kansas. Even though I missed mom and my two brothers, it was so hard to leave my dad. Once I was seated on the plane I couldn't hold back the tears. They flowed continually until the two hour flight came to an end.

Even as a woman, I was still dad's little girl and leaving him was always hard. Since the trip with my friends was over, I had to face the reality that awaited me back at home. I was heading back to a life of struggle with a drug selling and drug using alcoholic husband, whose presence was not a day to day guarantee. I loved my four children with all my heart, they were my heartbeat, but I wanted so much better for them. Instead, we lived in a home that should have been condemned.

Oh God, the offer dad made was so tempting but in my heart I knew I couldn't accept it. I somehow knew I could not leave Kansas and move to Maryland. At that point as we neared Kansas City International Airport, God spoke, "Teronda, your dad may get sick, may not be here always or be able to provide as he promised. But if you will allow me to be all that your dad promised, I will always be near you to provide. Just trust me with all that I have to provide for you."

I said, "Yes" to The Most High God and my testimony is "God has kept His word through lost jobs, foreclosure, repossession, no food, homelessness, abandonment and more." He never promised everything would be great, but He would always be present to make a way of escape and provision. This promise has carried me throughout my Christian walk. I chose to Abide in My Father's House and I could share many stories. My dad has passed away but God My Heavenly Father is now and eternally present as He promised.

Philippians 4:19
"But my God shall supply all your need according to his riches in glory by Christ Jesus."

God never promised

everything would be great,

but He would always be present!

Inspirational Thoughts

You are filled with excitement about your planned trip. Preparations have been made in ample time before the trip to save for the other expenditures. All details of the trip have been outlined and you have your complete itinerary ready to implement. The date of the trip gets closer and the excitement you had is no longer there. Other obligations take precedence over the trip and you must make a decision. How many times have you made plans and had to make a decision if you were going to continue with the plans or cancel the plans? Your heart says one thing but your mind states facts. So what do you do? You are filled with anxiety to the point you become sick.

The witness decided to go on the trip and once she got there she was relieved. She stepped out on faith. Once she arrived and confided in her dad, he made sure she would not need to worry about anything. Have you ever worried yourself sick or tossed and turned at night beating your pillow? Not knowing what to do and whom to turn too. And all the time someone was there willing to help you however they could. Isn't that what love is? That's the kind of love God gives to us daily; without questions, without answers, without reasons, without expectations, without judgments.

Your love ones want the best for you and they will do whatever they can while they can. But there are no guarantees they will be able to keep their promises. This is the reason you must depend on The Most High God. When you have God on your side He will never leave you nor forsake you, He will be with you always.

The witness learned as a new Christian to trust God. Even through her trials she knew The Most High God would never leave her. She stood on His promise and He made provisions. She chose to abide in her Father's house. What house will you abide in?

Maxine Williams Wright

"In *my* Father's house

are many **mansions:**
if it were not so,
I would have told you.

I go to **prepare** a place for you."

John 14:2

Psalm 73:26

"My flesh and my heart may fail, but God is the strength of my heart and my portion forever."

Maxine Williams Wright

CHAPTER 9

What is Faith?

PATRICIA M. GOINS
Columbus, Ohio

"What is Faith?" That is the question I asked myself as I sat in the middle row of the Metropolitan Baptist Church in Columbus, Ohio in June of 1996, just six months after my ex-husband and I were baptized. It was my second time getting baptized. I was 12 years old the first time and I honestly don't remember feeling anything special after being submerged in water. To be honest, I can't even remember why I decided to get baptized at the age of 12. However, in December of 1995 at the age of 26, I felt something completely different about my baptism experience. I remember feeling surprised and maybe even a little bit confused, as I watched a group of ladies surround me right before I was led into the baptism room. They were singing praises and telling me that the angels in heaven were celebrating my decision to be born again. December 31, 1995 also was my first time counting down to the New Year inside of a church.

After getting baptized the second time, I began attending bible study on Wednesday nights, hoping that I would learn more about this word called Faith. Was faith real? Could a person have faith about something, and it happen? Was the bible true? Was it true that with faith in God, anything was possible? These are the questions I found myself asking more and more everyday. It was during this time that I began asking God to show me what faith was. In 1999 my five-year marriage crumbled and I became pregnant outside the marriage. Pregnant with a one year old little girl on my hip and a seven year old son at my side feeling hopeless and lost, I decided to put God and the word 'faith' to the test.

I began making plans to leave Columbus, Ohio. I sold all my furniture and moved out of the apartment that my ex-husband and I once shared. I packed everything I could fit into my 1995 Mitsubishi Mirage, placed a prayer letter addressed to St. Matthews Publishing in the mail box, and my children and I drove to Cleveland, Ohio to stay with a friend from college. Unfortunately, after about two weeks, my daughter's constant crying was more than my friend's husband could take and I was told we had to leave.

At this point I had already given up my apartment and had no desire to return to my cheating and emotionally abusive relationship with my ex-husband, so I entered into the 30 day shelter at the Salvation Army in Cleveland, Ohio. When I think back to the period of time before my ex-husband and I split up, I now realize that when I was praying to God and asking Him to show me what faith was, He began giving me prophetic visions and dreams of what I would be going through in the future. I remember dreaming of being pregnant with one child while holding another. I remember dreaming of the shelter in Ohio and in Atlanta before my stays there ever actually happened. I guess God was warning me of what was to come.

When 30 days at the Cleveland shelter had ended, I knew that Cleveland, Ohio was not where I wanted to stay. One of the ladies at the shelter had been killed by a gang of women and my oldest son spoke of being mistreated at the school he was attending. It was at this time that I found myself at a crossroad. Do I return to Columbus, Ohio and to my ex-husband or go to a city where I have no family or friends? At the time, I was still haunted by the pain of my childhood abuse and my failed marriage, so I decided this was the perfect time to once again test this thing called faith. Despite all the women at the shelter who told me there was no way I would be able to make it in Atlanta with only $200 cash and 200 in paper food stamps, I decided to trust God. I wrote down the names of several shelters in Atlanta before setting out on my journey that would last 20 years.

Before moving to Atlanta in May of 1999, I had never written any books or sung in front of a crowd. Other than the flip pages I created as a child, I never even imagined I would become a film maker. I loved music but the thought of singing and performing in front of people would send me into a panic. I had stage fright so bad and I never viewed singing as more than a childhood dream. As a child I would stay up late at night and listen to the radio. I also would make stick cartoon characters and flip the pages so that the stick figures would move like a movie. I even designed clothing for my cartoon characters. But all of this was just childhood dreams and nothing I took seriously.

As soon as I arrived in Atlanta, I went to one of the shelters on my list. It was in the gymnasium of a church located on the corner of Moreland Avenue and Glenwood Road. The gym was filled with bunk beds and housed many homeless women and children. It seemed like hardships hit as soon as I arrived in Atlanta. The first night I was there, someone broke into my car and stole some of my belongings. As soon as I saw the broken car glass window, I went into hysteria. I was emotionally exhausted, three months pregnant, caring for two other small children, and in a city where I knew no one. I felt like I had made a big mistake and was doomed.

When your backup plan falls through, who do you turn to when you feel hopeless?

On one of my lists I had written down a lot of numbers. Next to one of the numbers I had written, "If all else fails call this number." Crying hysterically, I called the number hoping that someone would save us. The number was to a domestic violence hotline. The operator heard my hysteria and directed me to the nearest domestic violence shelter with open beds for a family of three. On the way to the shelter, my back tire blew out as I was getting on the freeway. I thought to myself, "Can things get any worse?" Suddenly a shiny red pickup truck pulled up behind us and out stepped a well-dressed African American man wearing a cowboy hat. "You need help Miss?" he asked smiling. I knew he was sent by God. This kind man put my spare donut tire on, gave me $20 dollars, and a card to his church.

When looking back over the last 20 years of my life, I realized that every time I was in a crisis something or someone would appear to help me and most of the time, these people were complete strangers. Once my children and I arrived at the Partnership Against Domestic Violence Shelter, I was finally able to relax. That year the section 8 housing list in Atlanta opened and I was able to apply. After three months at the Atlanta shelter, I transferred to Safe Haven Transitional, another shelter that allowed families to stay for a year. I ended up giving birth in the shelter, forming lifelong friendships, and getting my housing voucher.

Unfortunately, at that time I lost my faith due to hardships and instead of moving into a section 8 home in Atlanta, I ended up letting go of the voucher. I left Atlanta, returned to my ex-husband in Ohio and remarried him, which later ended up in yet another divorce. I remained in Columbus for another four years and found myself in another abusive relationship with a new man. I eventually decided to give Atlanta another try. After my second divorce and running from another bad relationship, I moved back to Atlanta. This ended up being a cycle that I would repeat over and over again over the course of 20 years. Anytime my faith became low I would run from Atlanta and move back to Ohio or Chicago. The battle was too tough, but anytime I would stay there and fight I would eventually arise victorious and move up the ladder in my creative career.

In 2019 after going through another fierce spiritual battle in Atlanta, I moved back home to Columbus, Ohio to lick my wounds and be around my family. My faith journey has been continuous. Will this be the end of me living in Atlanta? I'm not sure, maybe and maybe not. But the one thing I can say with certainty is that every step of the last 20 years of my life, God was always there. He always sent what I needed when I needed it most.

If someone had told me back in 1999 that taking that step of faith and leaving Ohio would lead to all the things that happened, I don't know if I would have left. If someone had told me that after moving to Atlanta, I would find out that my adopted sister lived there too, or that I would later move to Chicago, and then back to Atlanta, I would not have believed them. And that over the course of 20 years, I would write and self-publish seven books, write movie scripts, produce a short film, a feature film, and produce music with one of the top music producers in Atlanta, host radio shows that would reach millions, and have billboards with my picture and radio podcast on it all over Atlanta, I probably would have laughed and said "Yeah Right!" But that's exactly what happened. I saw a lot of my dreams come true, but I must admit that it wasn't without hard times and a lot of sacrifice.

God engineered us to survive.

The one thing I learned about faith is that faith does not guarantee that you will not experience pain or suffering. In fact, pain and suffering appeared to be some of the necessary ingredients of faith and character building. I believe that what faith does promise is that if you keep your trust in God, whatever you ask for in faith will be granted at God's perfect timing if you do not quit. I believe that faith is more about continuing to believe even when you face hard times, and even when it looks like there is no way the promise will be fulfilled. Faith is about trust, perseverance, belief, and putting in the work to get to the promise. Over the last 20 years I have seen some of my prayers and dreams come to pass. I will admit that there are prayers and visions that I am still waiting to manifest. I thank Maxine Williams-Wright for allowing me to give my testimony in her book. It has inspired me to start back writing and it has caused me to look at my time in Atlanta in a much different light. Check out my books and movies at www.patriciagoinsbooks.com.

My last words of advice are, if you want to truly understand the power of faith and you are standing at a crossroad trying to decide which road to take, I advise you to take the road less traveled. Take the road that's going to require you to use your faith. You never know where this untraveled road will take you, and what gifts, talents, blessings, and new friends you will discover along the way. My faith journey is far from complete. Every day that I open my eyes, I know that God is not done with me yet. Who knows what will happen with my next step of faith? So, my question to you is, if God asked you to take a step of faith in a completely different direction, and do something that is completely out of your comfort zone, would you do it, trusting Him to provide? How strong is your faith? What does the word "Faith" means to you?

Instagram: @PatriciaMarieGoins
Twitter: @ATWRadio
Facebook: www.facebook.com/patricia.goins.75
YouTube: www.youtube.com/user/Msgoins1119
www.patriciagoinsbooks.com
www.patrticiamariegoins.com
onthemoveshow@hotmail.com
www.blogtalkradio.com/patriciagoins

God always sent what
*I needed when I **needed** it most!*

Inspirational Thoughts

Spiritual battles will arise when you're chosen. When you have so much to offer the enemy wants to keep you from being the person The Most High God has destined you to be. Hardship is one of the avenues the enemy uses to keep you off balance. When you have hardship it's difficult to think about anything else beside basic survival. You resort to survival mode which consists of three modes: (1) Fight mode- you want to fight back or do something active to protect yourself. (2) Flight mode- you want to get away from the situation or avoid it. (3) Freeze mode- you often feel like you are unsure of what to do and you might shut down. Have you experienced any or all of the modes?

Life can surely place you in a state of distress. When you are in a hard place without resources it can be tempting to utilize unfavorable methods to unburden your situation, and to make decisions based on your temporary emotions. The Most High God is able to pull you from your hard place. Do you have unshakeable faith? Do you depend on God to fight your battles? That's what it takes when you are faced with extreme hardship. In the Old Testament Job referred to God using these words, "He may not come when I want Him, but He'll be there right on time." Even through Job's suffering he still did not give up on God. He had unshakeable faith.

When God has chosen you to serve Him, there will be many obstacles. The enemy knows your capabilities and must stop you. The enemy will use your friends, family, and church against you; he knows the gifts you have. When unknown problems occur they are usually from the enemy. Just know The Most High God will deliver you and get the glory. The witness came to terms with her purpose. Once you realize God has trusted you to work for Him; you know He has work for you to do and you are a force to be reckoned with. You must accept the fact that everyone is not going to love you, everyone is not going to *believe in you, and everyone is not going to support you. You have been distinctly designed the way you are for a reason. Your mold is only for you, so you must stay focused to complete God's assignments.*

I was able to relate to the witness because I've had some hardships during my journey. In order for me to do what God needed me to do, I had to lose to gain. The Most High God states in Jeremiah 29:11 "For I know the plans I have for you, declares the Lord, plans to prosper you and not to harm you, plans to give you hope and a future." I knew God was establishing my steps.

God hasn't forsaken you when you encounter setbacks. He's placing you on the path of your divine purpose and He had to move you to use you. I recommend that you take the advice of the witness. Get out of your comfort zone, take a leap of faith, and use the gifts The Most High God has given you. There may be some trials and hardships as you take a leap of faith but the arms of Jesus will catch you!

Where
would you be without
Faith?

Maxine Williams Wright

Testimonies
God's Unfolding Miracles

Philippians 4:13

"I can do all things through
Christ who Strengthens me."

Maxine Williams Wright

CHAPTER 10

You're My Third Call

MAXINE WILLIAMS WRIGHT
Marietta, Georgia

When I was younger I never had problems with employment. Salaries were substantial enough to support the needs and wants of myself and my sons after my second divorce. I managed to live in nice communities and surrounded them with meaningful and effective perceptions. I failed them when it came to teaching them how to pray and to study the word of God. I became a member of the Church of Church when I was in the 9th grade. The teachings stated you must be either hot or cold, being warm was frowned upon. In other words, you either lived without sinful acts or you were a sinner. I considered myself a sinner because there were things I did that were sinful. So I didn't go to church since that would have been hypocritical.

For about thirteen years I didn't go to church because I was afraid. I thought God would strike me down if I entered His holy temple. Fornication was sinful, drinking alcohol was sinful, and dancing was sinful; therefore I was a sinner. I recall the first time I danced I was a freshman in college. Two of my college girlfriends gave me a broom and showed me how to move my feet. I had never been to a party and had never danced with a boy. I chose not to attend the high school senior prom and high school senior graduation dance.

My parents were Baptists and didn't influence my decisions not to participate.

I discovered later in life it was okay to serve and worship God if you have imperfections. I must say the Church of Christ saved me during my teen years from many unknown and dangerous probabilities. My youngest son and I became members of Turner Chapel African Methodist Episcopal Church in Marietta, Georgia in 1995. By this time my oldest son was 17 years old and there was nothing I could do to get him to attend church with us. I asked God to forgive me for not teaching my sons how to worship and to serve during that period of separation from Him. Even though I was inactive and a non-member of a church, His presence never left me. The Most High God knew my potential, my worth, and the person He needed me to be. I had once served Him with all of me. I was His child and He knew me well. My summers were spent teaching bible study to children. My Sundays consisted of knocking on doors and sharing a word about God. I felt God's presence all around me.

Financial hardship struck me during my middle aged years. Somehow when I reached my mid 50s employers were not quick to offer employment opportunities. I knew my age was a factor but employers will never tell you that was the primary reason for no consideration is age discrimination. Why should they hire someone in their mid 50s when there were so many younger applicants?

I started substitute teaching to have a source of income and to keep my mind occupied. Plus I worked 15 part-time hours a week at a college but didn't receive compensation due to their financial instability. I subbed for several months at different schools and the longest assignment was at Marietta High School. I used my savings and credit cards to keep the household functioning. After I depleted my savings and maxed out my credit cards, I humbled myself before my family and friends. I had always been the giver and not the borrower. I didn't understand why I was going through such hardship.

For the first time in my life I had to ask for help. It took everything in me to ask my family and my ministry members for financial support. I recalled donating on many occasions to others in the ministry and to family members, but now I was humbled to the point of asking for financial support. I thought about giving up and walking away from everything and everybody. I wanted to get in my car and drive until I utilized my remaining resources. In other words, I wanted to disappear and just exist somewhere else. The only person I didn't want to hurt and to worry was my mother. She was the reason I stayed put. Those I had supported and assisted were not there for me but I managed to press on and thanked God for the hearts He touched who came to my rescue. I will forever be grateful.

---

*Trust in the Lord and closed mouths
will open, proud shoulders will lean on Jesus,
and love will be the reason.*

The Most High sent many angels to care for me. Friends who knew I wasn't working mailed checks to me and some placed cash in my hands when I saw them at church. One evening I was on my way home and saw a family on the side of road holding a sign. It truly touched my heart because it was a woman and man with their baby. The woman was holding the sign and the man was holding the baby. The sign read "Please help, trying to get home, we need gas and food." I stopped my car and gave them $5.00. When I got home later that evening my mailbox held a check for $500.00 with my name on it. I knew The Most High God was still using His chosen people to bless me. By sharing what I had God multiplied my act of kindness by one hundred.

During my time of working part-time and being unemployed I discovered many talents God had given me. I wrote my first play, created a collection of wall art, vases, and candleholders, and became an interior designer. I used those gifts from God as a source of income. It took stillness and unemployment to get my attention. Sometimes it takes an emphatic change in your life to direct you to your divine path.

The Pastor of my church knew I was experiencing financial hardship. He asked another church member who was in a position to assist me with employment. I was so grateful that my Pastor cared enough to think about my wellbeing. I was hired as a contractor and the assignment had potential to turn into a fulltime position, so I had confidence everything was going to be alright.

It felt good working a nine to five again. I shared an office with another member from church that the Pastor also recommended. We became really good friends and helped each other through our struggles. Some days were hard for me and she knew exactly what to say. Some days were hard for her and God guided my words just for her. Then after several months on the assignments we both were told that our assignments were over. I went into a state of panic but I managed to calm myself as I spoke with my coworker. When the time came I said my goodbyes and was back to seeking other options. I decided to focus on my creativity since that was a gift.

The first morning of being home without having to go to work, I went into my home office which was my favorite room. I sat there in silence and from the pit of my stomach a piercing squeal filled the room. I ended up on my knees in my bedroom beside my bed. I prayed like I had never prayed before. I screamed over and over to God, "I can't go back, I can't go back!" I couldn't go back to having nothing and feeling hopeless. I stayed there until I was exhausted. I managed to compose myself and went back into my office. I sat behind my desk dazed and motionless for a couple of hours. There was nothing else I could do, it was in God's hands.

I received a phone call from an unrecognized number. The woman asked, "May I speak to Ms. Wright?" I answered, "This is she." My mood was still somewhat solemn and I sat there waiting but didn't know what I was waiting on. My mind was empty, my spirit was drained, and yet my heart was beating. The woman began to talk about a position I had applied for, but I had no idea which position since I had applied for numerous positions. She asked if I still had an interest so I excitedly told her, "Yes," without knowing the position she spoke about because it had been too long ago. She then stated, "I have to fill this position today, I've called two other applicants but they didn't answer, you're my third call. Do you want the position?"

At that point I thought someone was playing on the phone, but I still accepted her offer. She hired me over the phone without an interview. She heard the excitement in my voice and I praised God while she was on the phone. I kept saying thank You God, I couldn't restrain myself. She calmly said, "Yes, it's okay to thank Him." She told me to report the next week to complete the new hire documents. I accepted the offer without knowing the details of the position since I didn't want her to know I didn't remember. After the call I researched and located the position which I had saved on my computer. I reported on the required date and time without knowing all the details of the position because it didn't matter since I knew it was a gift from The Most High God.

God heard my voice, saw my dire need, and felt my pain. The Most High God orchestrated the entire situation. He arranged for the two previous calls not to be answered, so I could answer the third call. I am so grateful for His favor!

Sometimes it takes an emphatic change in your life to direct you to your divine path!

Testimonies

God's Unfolding Miracles

Maxine Williams Wright

Inspirational Thoughts

The years you chose not to obey nor walked not by My side.
I told Gabriel to blow his horn to release the multitude of angels from beyond,
To cover you from the rising of the sun 'til the going of the same.
I knew you were confused,
Yet ashamed when you chose not to worship My Name.
I waited with open arms– extended hands,
You were in My plans.
After many wasted years you returned to My domain,
You needed shelter from the rains–
To wash away your stains.
I blew the winds upon your face to dry your tears,
To loose your fears.
I carried you through the storms– not a scratch on you was formed.
I relieved you from strife– prevented sacrifice.
I kissed your cheeks while you were asleep,
Placed a shield of protection from your head to your feet.
I told my servant to hire your name to sustain.
To keep you from going back...

2 Corinthians 12:10

"That is why, for Christ's sake, I delight in weaknesses, in insults, in hardships, in persecutions, in difficulties. For when I am weak, then I am strong."

Maxine Williams Wright

CHAPTER 11

Seeking My Purpose

DIANNE COGGINS
College Park, Georgia

It was a typical Monday for me. I pressed through the day not feeling so well. I was tired and weak. A year prior I was diagnosed with a goiter and thyroid disease. I was given an ultra sound and told to come back in a year. I was not prescribed any medication but I knew that having this disease would cause me to have symptoms of fatigue, and low energy. I was experiencing weight loss, irregular heartbeats and sweats (more than the usual menopause hot flashes).

I called my friend Vanessa whom I speak to three to four times a day. I told her that I was not feeling well and needed to lie down. She was out shopping and told me she would check in on me later. I decided to get a glass of water then head upstairs to my bedroom. As soon as I swallowed the water I immediately threw it up. The gagging was so severe it tightened the muscle in my heart to the point I could not breathe properly. I immediately called Vanessa back and told her what was happening and to come get me as soon as possible. She left the items in the checkout lane and drove to my house. I was doubled over in pain when she arrived. We headed for the nearest hospital which was Wellcare. Once in the lobby I was taken back to a private room and vital signs were taken. I was told that it would be a while before I could be seen because the waiting room was full to capacity.

We decided to drive to another hospital because I felt too bad and didn't want to wait. I needed to know what was happening. My children were contacted so they could meet us there. By the time we arrived at the second hospital I was in so much pain that I was scaring myself and Vanessa. Panic started to set in since I had never felt that kind of pain. I just knew I was experiencing a heart attack because it felt like a weight of 1000 lbs. was placed on my chest. Once in the lobby I was taken to a room where I had my vitals taken, IV inserted, blood work and other tests were run. I was admitted in a room with doctors and nurses all around me. As I laid there in the hospital bed, I reflected on the fact that I had not been in a hospital in 36 years. Not since the birth of my youngest child.

Lay your burdens down and get ready for your destiny ride.

I gave thanks to The Most High and vowed that whatever happens, will be His WILL. I will let go and let HIM take me through whatever was happening to me. I came to terms with whatever I was to go through. My children arrived and the fright on their faces made me desperate. Since I was so weak I was unable to put on my go-to "mom happy face" to appear that everything is alright. My oldest, Dan, took charge and questioned the doctors, asked for a breakdown of terms, what and why were certain things being done, called my sisters and friends. My children spent the night with me for three nights in the hospital and stayed around the clock. Their spouses and children had to regroup and find a way to get along without them. I did not have a heart attack. I was diagnosed with Graves' disease and Takotsubo Cardiomyopathy or broken heart syndrome (its stress induced, not a heart blockage). Once at home my son Dan notified all my friends and informed them not to contact me. Also, he took control of my cell phone. I was only allowed to eat, sleep, take my medications and watch

TV based on the orders of my son. My children took turns serving my meals, bathing me, giving me medications and taking me to scheduled doctor visits for the next three weeks.

This was by far the most life changing moment in my entire life. I am so appreciative of the relationship I have with my children. I often thought of the time when I would no longer be around and how they would cope without me. This incident has taught me that I raised intelligent, compassionate, responsible human beings. I look at life and my life very differently now. I was able to reflect on the many family members and friends that reached out to me, to offer a word, a meal or a phone call. I've come to an understanding how fleeting "TIME" is and has always been. No longer will I take anything for granted and I'm thankful for each breath and movement I take. I'm seeking my purpose and I'm not wasting "TIME" on the things that don't matter in my life. I praise The Most High God for His favor upon my life.

*I had to let go
and
let God!*

Inspirational Thoughts

God sends reminders that are unnoticed due to daily routines and challenges. Your good health allows you to complete your functions. Those routines can be interrupted abruptly when your body receives a massive, erratic disturbance. Your body has ways to communicate by showing abnormal signals to get your attention. Signals are often ignored when they warn you with a nudge. That same scenario often happens in your life. The tendency is to ignore God's warning signals and reminders. The Most High God shows you how and you take alternate routes filled with disparities. He makes known what He wants you to do, yet you think your decisions are better which leaves you confused. He tells you where to go but you have your own agenda that leaves you overwhelmed or out of your scope of moral principles.

Signals will speak loudly and precisely when they demand attention; they will not be ignored. Aren't you glad The Most High God loves you enough to warn you? Not only will He warn you, He will protect you. He will paint the canvas with all the colors needed to create His masterpiece, and you are that work of art. When you are in need He will cause others to get out of line and leave everything behind. He will cause sons to take control. He will cause families to enforce new regulations. In other words, He got you.

The witness realized how situations can become critical within moments. She was grateful for her relationship with her family and friends. She had unshakeable faith in The Most High God during her life changing condition. She refused to allow her condition to stop her from seeking her purpose. God saved her and extended her life for His purpose. There is much more work to be done to glorify The Most High God.

Seek and you shall find!

Maxine Williams Wright

Give God your **weakness**

and He'll give you His **strength!**

2 Thessalonians 3:3

"But the Lord is faithful, and he will strengthen you and protect you from the evil one."

CHAPTER 12

Unconditional Love

CATRINA RAVENEL
Douglasville, Georgia

This testimony is mostly about my son and my unconditional love. For the sake of privacy, instead of sharing his legal name, I will share with you what his name means. My son's name means "Son of strength and courage." I gave birth to my son while on an extended visit to the Holy Land of Israel. Here's our story.

I was pregnant with my second child and was in my first trimester when I was informed that my pregnancy was considered high risk. Three ultrasounds later and in the 4th month of pregnancy, my doctors were strongly recommending I terminate the pregnancy. According to my ultrasound test results, my placenta was filled with too much fluid, the fetus head was measuring larger than normal, a small calcium deposit was observed between the eyes and more than likely they said, my child was at risk of being born with mental retardation.

Needless to say, this news was dreadful and I was painfully saddened to say the least. However, once I regained my bearings, I directed my unapologetic attention and energy towards the doctors who dared to advise termination based on their mere human interpretation of my non-life threatening test results. Immediately, I requested a conference with the supervising physician. After, I shared with him the recommendation given to me by his staff, I stated that no one had the right to take my hope away! After all, you all are not God and I'll be keeping my baby! I had faith that God, not man had the last word and final say on the matter. I decided then and there not to accept the doctor's recommendation to terminate my pregnancy and decided to keep my baby!

Interesting how all this happened on the morning of 9-11. While exiting from my doctor's office visit around 9:00 a.m., I was walking through the lobby with tears streaming down my face when the breaking news happened to capture my attention. At that time, the upper portion of the World Trade Center was engulfed in fire and smoke. Including the news to terminate my pregnancy, it was the saddest day ever.

The following January, I gave birth to my handsome son. His height and weight were comparable to that of my first and third born children. Nonetheless, my son was diagnosed with macrocephaly and mild intellectual delay. As an infant, my son's ability to simply turn his head and body from side to side was challenging for him. Also, as he got older, crawling, walking and running was a challenge too. At the age of eight months, my son was referred to the Babies Can't Wait (BCW) program and assigned a physical, occupational, and speech therapist for intervention and support. Around the age of seven, my son grew taller, stronger and his equilibrium became increasingly steady and he also experienced less falls. My son's head size and body was now in normal range. Eventually he grew into his abilities leaving behind many disabilities. But the learning disabilities/cognitive delay remained present indicating my son would require special education.

While the school system helped with special education and speech therapy, my son would still need additional resources that the school system did not provide. I needed outside agency support but didn't know how to locate them. At the time, I turned to the elementary school social workers and teachers for advice but that wasn't their area of expertise. As time went on, I felt I had no other choice but to rely on myself. I enrolled in college and graduated with my social work degree hoping that would lead me to locate additional agency resources. I was always in search for more information and prayed one day I would come to understand the real cause behind my high risk pregnancy and my son's cognitive delay. I knew that everything in life happened for a reason, but what was the reason? What was God's reason for my son's learning disability? It would take another 15 years for me to receive clarity and understanding to these questions.

> *Whoever is wise, let him understand and whoever is discerning, let him know; for the ways of the Lord are right.*

In the meantime, I was determined to find additional resources and answers, just part of my DNA, I guess. Unfortunately, by this time, my health began to take a turn. I recall feeling extremely fatigued and my energy level was severely low. My energy was too low to run errands on the weekend but just enough to meet my employment responsibilities during the week. So every weekend, I was overwhelmingly exhausted, yet, still determined to conduct my research somehow. I listened to podcasts, lectures, and conferences on health while lying weak in my bed. It was during this time that I learned about the necessity of iodine supplementation especially during pregnancy. Iodine deficiency causes fatigue and an extreme iodine deficiency results in cognitive disabilities, learning disabilities, developmental disabilities, slow learning and a host of other health issues as well. Could this be the breakthrough I had been praying and searching for? Can the answer really be this simple? Well, I was on a mission to find out if this was the root of my son's learning disability and my extreme fatigue. I placed my first order of iodine supplements. Due to both our health conditions, I came to the realization that both my son and I must have been severely iodine deficient! Finally, I had some viable information to work with and decided to supplement my son and myself with iodine and selenium.

(Iodine deficiency during pregnancy is serious for both the mother and the baby. It can lead to high blood pressure during pregnancy for the mother and mental retardation for the baby. Iodine plays an important role in development of the central nervous system. In extreme cases, iodine deficiency can lead to cretinism, a disorder that involves severely stunted physical and mental growth.)

(Selenium a mineral found in the soil. Naturally appears in water and some foods. While people only need a very small amount, selenium plays a key role in the metabolism. Selenium has attracted attention because of its antioxidant properties. Antioxidants protect cells from damage. It is important to take selenium to support the thyroid when also taking iodine.)

There was no exact protocol to use as a guide for my son and me. I was totally on my own. I didn't know what the overall outcome would yield, but I was determined to experiment and figure it out. I ordered several books on iodine. I also ordered seaweed (an iodine food source), a bottle of J. Crows Lugol's Iodine in tincture form and a selenium supplement to support the thyroid while taking iodine. It wasn't long at all before my energy levels soared. In a very short amount of time, I was able to resume normal activities again. The next summer, I was on a kick ball league. Surprisingly, another benefit I noticed was my dilemma with hemorrhoid episodes finally disappeared. That was four years ago and they have never returned. During this time, my son was experiencing his own iodine benefits.

I began administering iodine and selenium to my son when he was approximately 15 years old and in high school. I must admit, my son experienced amazing results! Oh my goodness, this was it! I found the missing mineral deficiencies! Here's what happened next. At least two weeks into my son's iodine supplementation program, his results constantly unfolded.

My first observation was when my son took the initiative to do his homework. I usually had to ask my son if he had homework. This was already a positive benefit. The second observation was when my son asked me for assistance with identifying 20 geometric shapes. I referred him to YouTube to complete his assignment and he successfully completed it. It was the next school day, when my son's teacher asked for a volunteer to raise their hand and identify four geometric shapes. My son reported that after several students were struggling to come up with the answer, he raised his hand and with confidence identified the hexagon, octagon, pentagon and nonagon shapes. Already, I was impressed witnessing my second indicator to the benefits of iodine. It was unbelievable.

---

*Victory comes to those
that seek understanding.*

My third observation occurred at home when my son handed me a beautiful sketch that he drew of Bart Simpson on a plain piece of paper. Now, I know my son's typical attempts at art which consisted of stick people using straight lines for body parts and circles for heads. But, now I'm looking at a full body sketch of Bart Simpson. Maybe I misunderstood my son so I asked, you meant you traced it, right? Again, my son said, "No mom, I drew it." Come to find out, he was following a sketch artist on video and duplicated the exact image. I was more than impressed. I was speechless. Wanting to convince me further, my son sketched out a teddy bear holding a heart this time. This was divine intervention at best. I was so elated, I even posted the sketches on my Facebook page.

The iodine was working! My son had been constipated since birth and after using iodine for just a short period of time, it drastically improved. I knew what was happening at home with my son's cognitive improvement and other health benefits, but I was curious as to what was happening at school. I was curious to know if his teacher had noticed any improvement. A day or two later, my son's teacher was calling me on the phone. She seemed excited while she reported that my son had the highest class grade on his geometry test and of course I was excited too! This was the call I had been waiting for.

By the end of the week, my son came home with more good news and a new high school T-shirt that his teacher gave him as a reward for his behavior in class. Of course, I wanted to hear every detail of the events that took place in class. My son went on to explain how his head teacher left an assistant teacher in charge of the class while she stepped away. The head teacher returned to her class only to learn that her entire class had been misbehaving. My son was the only student with exceptional behavior. Wow, the iodine helped him to stay focused in the midst of chaos.

I wanted to know from my son just exactly what he had focused his attention to when all the chaos was going on in the classroom. My son replied, that he was studying for the next geometry test. Here I was again, surprisingly shocked. Yes! I was witnessing more iodine results. The next day, I asked my son how his test went and he replied, "I got 100%, mom!" My son was happy to get his new T-shirt and I was happy witnessing the benefits of my research at work. The iodine was stimulating the neurons in his brain and releasing toxins too.

In 2020, my son graduated high school and was highly recommended by his teacher to participate in the STEP (School to Employment Program). My son is very high functioning and helpful around the house too. He performs daily chores and has responsibilities like any teenager. He also babysits his niece and nephew at times without adult supervision. In our home our family relies a great deal on my son. In retrospect, it was 15 years ago when I asked the Most High, why was my son born with special needs? The answer revealed to me was this, "That you, my child can spread the message about the necessity and the benefits of iodine and other essential minerals to my people! This will be your mission, your gift, and your purpose."

I am humbled beyond measure. I continue to conduct extensive research on health and mineral deficiencies and one day will write my book and share my work to help others on their healing journey. I am truly thankful and grateful I listened to the Most High instead of taking my doctor's advice on the morning of 9-11-2001. By the way, I eventually discovered that I was severely zinc deficient which resulted in my son's large head circumference at birth. Unfortunately, prenatal vitamins don't always contain iodine or enough iodine along with other essential minerals needed for both mom and embryo.

In closing, according to my research, there are millions of children worldwide who are born with severe iodine deficiency resulting in mental retardation, low IQ, ADD, ADHD or are extremely short stature and most parents have no knowledge of this occurrence and sometimes give birth to two or three children with the same issue due to the same deficiency. Parents and grandparents it's really up to you to give your children and/or grandchildren the gift of iodine in the form of kelp, cod liver oil, or Lugols iodine. Help develop their brain while significantly increasing their IQ. You will be amazed at the outcome. I pray this testimony will provide you with all the "strength and courage" you need on your healing journey.

"In order for human beings to reach their maximum potential, they need iodine."

Iodine:J. Crows Lugols formula/Ioderol tablet 12.5 mg
Selenium: A plant based mustard seed source by Globalhealing.com

I am *truly* thankful
and grateful I listened
to The Most High God!

Testimonies

God's Unfolding Miracles

Maxine Williams Wright

Inspirational Thoughts

Have you ever been filled with nothing but joy and then receive news to reverse your joyfulness to gloom? You try to make sense of the situation, but your mind is unable to grasp for answers, for resolutions, for clarity, and for hope. You realize that you can't depend on others to provide answers for your problems. You know within your spirit God equipped you with resources to seek the knowledge needed for your situation. You discover resolutions to bring about life changing effects that will become beneficial. You step out on faith to govern the fate of the loved ones embedded within your heart. You pray for guidance, for discernment, and for precision. You see meaningful results from your determination. You reap the reward of your determination; now you know your sacrifice was not in vain because God indeed heard your prayers. Not only do you behold the reward, others are affected and others witness the miraculous changes.

When you exult unconditional love there's nothing you won't do. The unconditional love the witness had for her son equipped her with knowledge and placed her on a path to enlighten others. The same unconditional love God has for you. The Most High God sent His son to demonstrate His love. Jesus came willingly to show His unconditional love. As the quote says, "actions speak louder than words." Man had given up on the witness' son, but God did not. Man has admiration for perfection. God has purpose for imperfection, He will use to bring glory to His name and to build His kingdom. Will you allow God to use your imperfections?

1 Chronicles 16:11

"Look to the Lord and his strength; seek his face always."

Maxine Williams Wright

CHAPTER 13

God Is...

T.S. EDWARDS
Atlanta, Georgia

Who would have thought after surviving sexual abuse, physical and mental abuse, all before the age of 18 that my life could get worse? Well, it did. But God proved that He would never be less than His word. He will always bring joy in times of sorrow. He will carry me when I can't walk any further.

Let me explain:

It was a late Sunday afternoon. I was lounging around my apartment, dreading going to work the next day. Being a 19 year old black female in the military far from home, in a job that was 98% male, brought many challenges. I literally hated my job. Wait, that's not entirely true. The job was fine, it was the people that made it hell. So as I mentally prepared for the hell I was going to face Monday morning, my phone rang. I recognized the number of my favorite uncle. I was immediately irritated but curious at the same time. I was saying to myself, "He better be calling to apologize after all this time!" Even though he was my favorite uncle and more like a father, we were estranged at the time.

About a year prior we had gotten into a huge argument at his house because he didn't like the man I had recently married. He felt that my new husband wasn't the right man for me and I was too young to be married. He even assaulted my new husband that day. But in my mind, I was grown, making my own money, and I could make my own decisions. Who was he to tell me what to do? So I stormed off, vowing to never speak to him again until he apologized, and I did. My uncle was extremely stubborn, and I had learned early on because of past trauma experiences as a child, how to disconnect feelings.

It's best to know when to let go,
when to walk away, and when to yield.

Needless to say, a year passed and neither one of us had picked up the phone to converse. So I answered the phone with a slight attitude. In less than a minute of talking to him my life seemed to stop. He informed me that my mother was involved in an accident and was in a coma. I felt as if I was having an out of body experience and I could see myself falling to my knees in slow motion. I could hear myself cry out uncontrollably, "Nooooooo!" But it felt like I was watching a movie. In my mind, I didn't want to believe it. It wasn't real. It couldn't be real. She has to be alright. God is a merciful God. God is light in darkness. God had brought me through some already horrifying moments. Would God leave me now? Would God take away the one person who I depended on to give me purpose? I had to believe that God wouldn't put any more on me than I could bear. So I got myself together and headed home to take care of my mother. She never regained consciousness, and in less than a month, God called her home.

As I buried my mom at the age of 19, I also buried my purpose for life. I could not wrap my head around how God took the one person who loved me. I felt God had forsaken me and I slipped further and further into darkness. I became more and more depressed. Also during this time, I was feeling ill all the time, so I thought. I soon discovered that I was pregnant. When I found out I was pregnant I

Maxine Williams Wright

should have felt terrified. I was a young black female in the military, all alone, far from any family, still grieving the loss of my mother and now pregnant. But I didn't instead I felt a sense of calmness come over my entire body because I was now not alone.

Even though God called my mother home, she was my purpose for life. He had now given me this beautiful life that I was responsible for. I now had a renewed sense of purpose for my life. My unborn child reminded me that…

> **God is** love.
> **God is** always by my side and will never forsake me.
> **God is** my light in the middle of darkness.
> **God is** my joy during times of sorrow.
> **God is** life.
> **God is** and will always be my Footprints in the Sand.

T.S. Edwards
Author of…
The Adventures of Hilde and Carlos: We are going to Paris
The Adventures of Hilde and Carlos: We are going to Guam
Articles Of Life, A Collection of Short Memoir Essays of Managing Life
www.TSEdwardsAuthor.com
IG: @tsewards_author

God **brought** *me through!*

Testimonies
God's Unfolding Miracles

Maxine Williams Wright

Inspirational Thoughts

When you become a young adult you often think you are ready for the world. Ready to take on all life has to offer. Ready to create your own path. Ready to enforce your plan. Ready to conquer anything that stands in your way. Youthfulness produces empowerment and nothing can alter your concept, your mission, and to keep you from the finish line. Life has a way of throwing unexpected curve balls that will cause you to miss. You thought you were ready until the ball hits you. You quickly learn you need more than just you to handle sudden adversities.

The witness was young and filled with aspiration. She was her own woman making her own decisions. How many times have you put on a piece of God's armor ready for battle? In order to be ready to handle life changing situations you need the whole armor of God. A piece of God's armor will not equip you for what you are to face. When you suit up in God's armor you will be ready for battle. There are so many battles you can encounter such as the loss of loved ones, loved ones becoming ill, financial hardships, addictions, wayward children, troubled marriages, church politics, on the job challenges, and others. The witness was faced with the loss of her mother and her purpose for life. Have you ever questioned God and asked, "Why?" I think we all have. The witness realized the love God had for her. Though she had lost her mother, God gave her a new life and a new purpose for life. How many times have you felt defeated? Maybe you thought there was no other place to go, no other hand to play, no other move to make. And just like that, God has a ram in the bush to save you. Glory to God!

1 Corinthians 16:13

*"Be on your guard; stand firm in the faith;
be courageous; be strong."*

Maxine Williams Wright

CHAPTER 14

Why I Celebrate Two Birthdays

COSSETTA TAYLOR
Mableton, Georgia

I started having so much pain in my abdomen that I had to go to the doctor. We were in the Air Force and the doctors on base were treating me for ulcers. The prescribed medications weren't helping me at all, so I found me a civilian doctor, who after examining me immediately recommended me to a gynecologist. He found adhesions on my fallopian tubes and cysts on my ovaries. He called a conference with my husband and me and recommended surgery to remove them.

On Thursday April 8th, 1971 my husband Larry dropped me off at Tampa General Hospital for a common surgery. While the doctors performed the surgery, they discovered they needed to remove my appendix as well. It isn't clear what went wrong, but I stopped breathing and was pronounced dead. After my surgeon cleaned up he came over and stood beside me. As I laid covered on the table he began to tap me on the arm while asking, "Sweetheart, how could you do this to me?" I shocked the doctor when I asked, "Do what?" He called out to the staff and nurses and they came running. They were surprised to find me awake.

Several amazing things were going on at the same time! No, I did not experience "going into the light!" However, I do remember feeling extremely cold! The first thing I remember after the extreme coldness was the nurses wrapping me in a bandage and pulling my flesh tightly together. Since they pronounced me dead I had not been stitched or stapled back together properly. They had planned to perform an autopsy to learn the cause of death.

---

*The only authority over
your life comes from God.*

Amazingly, after time passed I healed without the usual scar of the stitches or staple marks. It looked as if I just had a scratch down my stomach. It was a blessing that my husband wasn't there to sign my body over to a funeral home that day. Had I been embalmed they would have killed me without knowing I was still alive.

Years later I think I finally understood why I was given another chance at life. His word said "Every ear must hear!" I had been in church my entire life but now I know how God really wants me to live! I also realize that He has work for me to do for His kingdom! I choose to make the most of my experience by celebrating two birthdays!!!

*I was pronounced dead
still I live!*

Inspirational Thoughts

When a doctor makes an incision into your body that's life threatening, it becomes simple or complicated. The doctor discovered another issue while he performed the surgery. Once they probe into your body it's possible something was missed prior to the observation. God doesn't need to probe, He aims directly at the target area and hits a bullseye every time.

Suppose The Most High God performed surgery on you. He opens you up and finds all kinds of hazardous conditions which He knows are there. He might need to make some small and some deep incisions, some stitches, some patches and some blood transfusions. You trust God enough because you know He is the creator and knows exactly what you need. He knows what to take away and He knows what to put in. He will remove obstacles that will hinder you from being the person He needs you to be. He will humble you to stand taller. He will insert the blood of Jesus in your veins. He will regulate your heart.

God awaken the witness, He needed her to complete her unfinished assignments. The doctors performed the routine surgery and there was a mishap. But isn't that how life is? From day to day there are unforeseen occurrences. That's why it's beneficial to have a relationship with The Most High God. If you are lifeless, he will provide life to dead situations. If you are choking, He will clear your passageway. God is here to awaken you. If you don't have a life insurance policy with Him, you need to call Him now. He's available 24x7 wherever you are!

Habakkuk 3:19

"The Sovereign Lord is my strength; he makes my feet like the feet of a deer, he enables me to tread on the heights."

Maxine Williams Wright

CHAPTER 15

Why Not Run

COSSETTA TAYLOR
Mableton, Georgia

Every now and then, while sitting on my favorite pew at church, the urge to get up and take a run around the church will overtake me. With each lap around I give God my praise! I might look foolish to those who don't know my story, but in 2001 I experienced a severe depression after burying my son on his 18th birthday. My only brother died a few months later and my mother died three weeks after my brother. I was put on different medications and before long I was on 16 different pills a day! My body started to shut down.

I was in a wheelchair for almost three years and couldn't bathe myself or get dressed without help. Also, I was on oxygen 24/7 and had to drag an oxygen tank around everywhere I went. I wasn't able to do the things that I loved to do. I couldn't teach my Sunshine Band any longer, I couldn't teach the cooking classes, or teach public speaking and drama to my 4-H club. I was no longer able to direct the children's choir! "Lord, I've got to get up from here" was my cry from deep inside to The Most High God.

> *You must have the willingness in your heart to serve God.*

One day as I laid on my bed I began to just talk to God. I said, "Lord there is still ministry in me. I want to continue to serve you and I can't do it from 6 ft under. Today I am leaving it up to you. Raise me up please, or take me home. I don't want to live like this." I fell asleep but when I woke up God begin to teach me how to come off each medication. He directed my path and my life began to change. Soon I was able to bathe myself and I could dress myself with just a little help. I started walking around my home using the family room and dining room like an inside track. Eventually, I was able to get out of the house and went to our local Meijer department store. I pushed the shopping cart around in the store instead of my walker for an hour every day.

Later I started using a cane and walked in the mall. Finally, I gave the cane away. I graduated from the wheelchair to a walker, to a cane, and to walking on my own. So YES, I'm excited when he allows me to take a run!

God directed my **path** *and my* **life** *began to change!*

Maxine Williams Wright

Inspirational Thoughts

Do you ever think about the goodness of God and it makes you run, shout, dance, sing, cry, or laugh? Or maybe you do them all. No one knows your story but you. When you've never been through anything difficult you probably can't relate when you see someone praising The Most High God. There are many ways to praise. Some may sit quietly shaking their heads, some may hum, some may rock back and forth, some may tap their feet, some may raise their arms, and some may yell hallelujah. However the way you want to give God the glory, your praise does not require permission.

When the referee starts his count to ten you are certain that you are finished. Your health goes from bad to worse and all you can do is talk to your God. The witness had a little talk with her Lord and before the referee finished his count to ten, The Most High God stopped the count. He was not done with her yet because there was much more work to be done, many more souls for her to encourage, many more roles for her to play, many more children to direct, and many more lessons to teach.

Just remember, God is just a whisper away. Get to know Him, establish a relationship with Him. Tell Him all about it and He'll make it better by and by. All things work for your good. Trust Him enough to run.

Run for your purpose, run for your life, run for others in your life, run for humanity!

Ephesians 6:10

*"Finally, be strong in the Lord
and in his mighty power."*

Maxine Williams Wright

CHAPTER 16

Man said "NO" God said "Yes"

COSSETTA TAYLOR
Mableton, Georgia

I'm not certain just how it happened because I was too young to remember. Grandma always boiled Faultless starch to use when she ironed Grandpa's shirts. Somehow the pot spilled on my shoes. When my grandmother and grandpa removed my shoes and socks the skin from my ankles peeled off too! It was an awful sight to see a two year old in such agonizing pain. I still remember the scabs on my feet from the boiling starch and the scars remain as of today.

Throughout my lifetime I heard the story over and over about how the doctor informed my family that I would never walk again. My paternal grandmother, Big Momma Annie Mae, lived on the other side of town. She would walk to our house twice a day just to change the dressings on my feet. Needless to say, my ankles and feet did heal despite the doctor's prognosis. I learned to walk again and ran track from 7th grade through my freshman year in college. I even played basketball. Isn't God good? The doctors said, "NO," but He said, "Yes!"

My scars *remind* me
how *much* God loves me!

Testimonies
God's Unfolding Miracles

Maxine Williams Wright

Inspirational Thoughts

Childhood trauma can cause lifetime effects. Physical scars are more visible and unpleasing to the eyes. But what about psychological scars, the trauma you can't see? The invisible shattered pieces that haven't been stitched are the scars that torment your wellbeing. How many scars do you have? How many do you hide?

The witness was indeed blessed to be able to walk especially after the doctors said she would never walk again. This is just another case where The Most High God stepped in and turned the situation around. When God has outlined your path, nothing will keep your feet from walking. It might take you longer to reach your mark, but you will reach it. Life issues can get in the way of your life. No matter the deterrence, never, ever stop giving God the glory.

Your scars will remind you of the favor God has over your life. Reveal your scars to help others to see their scars differently. Your scars can save lives!

Walk
with
purpose!

Psalm 29:11

"The Lord gives strength to his people; the Lord blesses his people with peace."

Maxine Williams Wright

CHAPTER 17

A Survivor's Story

COSSETTA TAYLOR
Mableton, Georgia

I was only five years old when my step father would take me into our apple orchard and rub his penis over my genital area. I would cry as he kept asking me if it felt good. I just hated living with my mom because I didn't know how to tell her what happened since he kept telling me that she would whip me if she found out. I was never to tell!

One time when we all went fishing together, I had fallen asleep in the car and I woke up to him pulling my panties down. When I started to scream, he left me alone. That was the day that I asked my mom if I could go back living with my grandmother. Grandma was so mean, but I did not like my stepdad touching me at all. I had to choose the lesser of the two evils!

I knew that I had to be very careful with my Grandma because she would whip me for the slightest little thing. If I was smiling she had a reason to lash out at me. If I wasn't smiling she would hit me. Lord knows sometimes I would be afraid to even breathe! The one thing I knew to do was to get good grades! She believed in good grades and she said that every girl should know how to play the piano and how to do math! I had no problem with any of those requirements. I just didn't know how to get past her being so mean to me. I always had extra work when my friends were out playing. I couldn't visit anyone else's home unless she went as well. Many times while growing up there would be activities at school that I couldn't attend, especially if it involved boys being there. I did get to go to our 8th grade ball and to the homecoming dance when I was in the 11th grade! I think it was because I was both Homecoming Queen and Miss Lincoln High during my junior year in high school.

Grandma was so mean to me that when my first husband asked me to marry him after my first year in college, I said, "Yes." I just needed to get away and to be on my own! (That was a big mistake on my part.) I wanted to keep house and cook and decorate and shop on my own. Even with the pre-marital counseling, I found out that I was not ready for the sexual experiences that came naturally for most people, until after we were married. My God, I really wasn't ready for sex. I didn't realize it at the time but I could have used some more counseling.

Needless to say, it caused much pain throughout my marriage. My first husband Larry was still young and sex was everything to him. He didn't know how to be patient with me or how to help me to learn to love him sexually. I needed so much more than he understood or even desired to give me. All I knew was, I said, "I DO." That meant for better or worse, and it meant till death do us part! I had made a vow and I meant to keep it so I suffered through so much pain.

I cried so many days and nights but was overjoyed when I found out two years later that I was carrying our first baby, a little girl. However, she was born prematurely and only weighed 2 lbs. I was devastated when she passed away three days later. I named her Raina because it was raining that day, and all my dreams seemed to be rained on. Larry was saddened too, however, he did not fail to say mean hateful things to me as if it were my fault.

My sister gave birth to her first child the December of the previous year. Donnie was a healthy little boy and was doing well. It was October, Raina was born and had died, three days later, leaving us with an empty crib and broken spirits. Maybe Larry just needed to lash out at something or someone and I was the closest one to him. All I knew was it tore at my core when he looked at me and said, "You can't even have a baby. Your little sister had a baby and you can't even do that!" I was so crushed. It hurt badly to know I just couldn't satisfy him in any way.

Needless to say, I stayed with him, knowing he was cheating on me and constantly dating other women which he never kept a secret. I was constantly told how "bad" I was in bed and how "good" other women made him feel. I tried to please him but I just couldn't, so maybe he was right.

Time passed by and a year later I found out I was pregnant again. I didn't know whether to be happy or not. Larry had not changed his behavior toward me but he seemed glad that I was pregnant. But why did he keep going out with other women? One night a car drove into our carport, a woman got out of the car and came to the door for Larry. He told me to go into the bedroom and just stay there. He begged me not to come out. I was so scared and did as he had asked. I couldn't hear much of their conversation but he left with her. I really didn't know what to do. I had no family in Florida. I was friends with a few ladies on the base but we had bought a house and lived out in Progress Village, a suburb of Tampa. I had met some of the people at church but we had only attended a couple of months, so I didn't really know them. All I could do was pray but it was such a long night.

The next evening was "Love Feast" services at our church. I got dressed and went. I walked to the church but it was too dark for me to walk home alone. Larry had not returned home and I was still scared to be there alone. One of the older women at the church noticed me and asked if everything was okay. I told her that my husband was away and I was a little scared being home alone. She looked at me and said, "Honey, you can come and stay with me tonight. Mr. Ginyard is a longshoreman and will be gone for a few more days. I would love some company." I was so glad she said that and quickly agreed to go home with her. I didn't have anything with me to sleep in and wanted to go home to get something but she said I could just sleep in one of her gowns. She didn't want to inconvenience the deacon that was giving us a ride. I said, "Thank you."

We had a wonderful evening sitting there talking and eating a dish of ice cream before we went to bed. The bed felt so comfortable and I was able to actually enjoy a good night of rest. The next morning when she called me for breakfast I got up and the sheets were bloody. I was ashamed to have bled on them and apologized to her. She interrupted me and said, "But aren't you pregnant?" She had brought me back into reality. Yes, I was pregnant and needed to call my doctor. I felt fine but something was wrong. We got in touch with the doctor and he wanted to see me right away.

One of the members of the church, Sister McPherson, was a retired nurse. She lived next door to Mother Ginyard and did not hesitate to volunteer taking me to the doctor. After he examined me, Dr. Ayers decided I was threatening a miscarriage. I was told to go home and get off my feet. I was not to even walk to the bathroom if I didn't have to. What was I suppose to do? God only knew where Larry was! That's it! I am calling home!

Trust in the Lord with all your heart
and lean not on your own understanding.

I called home. Mama said, "Come home, baby!" I did just that, but first I got permission from my doctor to fly home. He said I should be okay since it was a rather short flight from Tampa, Florida to Greenville, Mississippi. I went home without Larry, without a job, with very little money and pregnant. It was not an easy pregnancy because I was sick all day. I found a very good doctor to continue my prenatal care. I kept losing weight because I couldn't keep any food down. I kept taking the vitamins and only could manage to keep a little 7 Up on my stomach for a little while.

Even dealing with the constant nausea and vomiting, I managed to be in good spirits. Until one day when I overheard mom's new man talking to her and saying that now that I was living there the bill for having the baby would be on them. I was crushed because I never, ever wanted to be a burden to anybody. So I immediately got the number for a free hospital in Mound Bayou, Mississippi. It was an all black city at one time and about 40 miles from Leland where we lived. They quickly accepted me as a patient and I actually had one doctor's appointment before the baby decided to make his way into the world. He was premature and weighed in at 4 lbs. even.

I was so glad to bring him home and take care of him. He was so precious and began to thrive right away. I had another surprise when I came home three days later from the hospital. Larry had sold the house in Tampa and moved back home to Leland. I wasn't sure about us being back together again so he stayed at his mom's and I stayed with mine. I did, however, agree to let him accompany me to baby Larry's first check-up. I was so glad he was with me when the doctor told us he had a heart murmur. He had been born with part of the left ventricle missing. We had moved back to Mississippi but the doctors sent us to Memphis, Tennessee to the Le Bonheur Children's Hospital. It was the best children's hospital for his care. (That's another journey in my life!)

Larry and I decided to get back together. Things were okay at times but he soon was back to his old ways. Women, women and more women! We ended up moving to Chicago, Illinois where Larry, Jr. continued medical treatment with a pediatric cardiologist and a pulmonary specialist at the Presbyterian St. Luke Hospital.

Almost seven years had passed when I was blessed with my very own little girl! She arrived a little early but weighed 6 lbs. She had breathing problems and we soon found out she was a severe asthmatic. Two years later I had Jesse who was a chronic asthma patient. There I was with three sickly children and a husband who was unfaithful! Thank God I had my faith in Him!

Then came a day I never dreamed would happen to me. I took an afternoon nap after I had put the babies down for a nap. Larry, Jr. was already nine years old and decided he would leave out of the house without permission. When I woke up I went into the bathroom to wash my face and noticed that someone had dropped the tissue holder into the toilet. When I bent over to take it out I noticed shoes… there was a man standing in the doorway!

I was so afraid and asked him what he wanted. He approached me as if to rob me as he pushed me into my bedroom asking for whatever money I had. He made me sit on the bed while he rummaged through the drawers and searched my purse and even my jacket. He told me to get up and began pushing me down the hallway into the back of the house. As we got closer to my family room, I sensed he had plans to rape me so I started thinking of what I could use as a weapon. At the same time I didn't want him to hurt my children and I was afraid they would wake up. He seemed like he was possessed or something and it wouldn't take much for a man like that to kill me and my children.

As we neared my sofa I felt it was now or never, so I tried to overtake him to take the knife he was holding on me away from him, but he was too strong. He knocked me onto the sofa and began hitting me in the face and mouth with the butt of the knife. I told him my husband would be home in a few minutes but he said, "No he won't. He never comes until late at night." He tore my clothes off and prepared to rape me, but as soon as he got his penis next to my body he released himself. He looked at me and in a very demonic voice said to me, "You're going to tell." I said, "Tell who." He kept saying, "You're going to tell." I kept trying to assure him that I wouldn't tell anybody. Just as he held the knife above me there was a rap on the window up front. I pushed him with all the strength I had and ran for the front door. (To run from the back of my house to the front was almost a half block. This was a ten room house with all rooms on the same floor.) It was Larry! I was out of breath as I pointed to the back of the house saying, "Man in back!" Larry took off running only to find that the man had gone out the back door and escaped into the alley. He called

Maxine Williams Wright

911 and got an ambulance for me and called the police.

I spent the next three days in Englewood Community Hospital where they tended to my wounds and offered rape counseling. I did not realize my hand had been cut during the struggle. My face was not a pretty sight and front teeth were both broken! What had I done to deserve such treatment? I wasn't allowed to go home alone. ECHO, an organization that works with rape victims called to arrange for someone from their organization to come into the home with you to see how well you are doing. They let Larry know when they would be bringing me home and asked him to be there. He was there and immediately put his arms around me to comfort me and welcome me home. The children were at his brother's house so we were alone after the couple from ECHO left. Larry started right away to put me through the entire rape all over again! It was awful.

Not long after that experience, I went to Michigan to visit with my sister. After being there a week, Larry and I talked and he said he thought it was over and I really didn't need to come back. It didn't matter too much to me since he was still being unfaithful. Of course I cried at first and felt so alone; the biggest hurt was I failed. I never like failing at anything. I just sat there numb from the inside out. A thousand thoughts ran through my mind. What would I do? No job, three children and no place to live! My sister had a husband and six children, and our living together wouldn't work for long, even though they would try to make me feel welcome. Finally, I gained the courage and strength to go upstairs and talk to my sister, Jennifer. She was always so feisty and quick to speak her mind! It was no surprise when she told me I didn't need him anyway. She was so tired of seeing me struggle to hold a marriage together just so my children would have a father around. She did make me feel better.

When we finished talking I knew I could make it on my own. I just needed to trust God! For once in my life I thought I didn't need a man in my life. The "I do" wasn't worth the pain I had experienced. After all, the 'till death do us part' and the feelings of LOVE had long been dead. And, I suppose TRUST had never been fully alive in my marriage in the first place! This was the Beginning of a New Chapter in MY Life!

For the first time in my life I had to get social services to help with supporting my children. I had heard so many stories about not being able to get help unless you lied about what you had or if you had family that could possibly help that they wouldn't help you. It wasn't like that at all. I filled out the application, they checked with Illinois to make sure I wasn't receiving any help from them and quickly approved my application. They gave me emergency food stamps and a list of places to go for housing assistance. I saw the perfect little house with a fenced in yard on the way there, so we stopped and got the information on renting it on the way back to my sister's house. I was able to get that house. We didn't have furniture but other members of our family who lived in Lansing were happy to donate different items that they were no longer using. God was so good!

Because I started to receive food stamps, I was offered classes from the EFNEP program. EFNEP stood for the Expanded Food and Nutrition Program. The young lady who came to my house gave me a pre-test to see how much knowledge I had about food and nutrition. I aced every test she gave me. She was so impressed with my scores that she told me they were in need of more people to go out and teach others how to choose good nutritious foods and how to budget the money they received from assistance. I was truly interested and called the agency to get an interview. I was scheduled for the next day and could hardly sleep the night before due to the anticipation.

Assurance has been placed over your life.

Maxine Williams Wright

I arrived early for my interview and was able to relax a bit before I went in to the room with six people who conducted the interview. That was the first time I was ever interviewed by more than one person at a time. The interview went well even though I was a bit concerned when they told me they were conducting interviews for the next two weeks and would let me know of their decision after they were finished. I thanked them and went back home. I had given them my sister's phone number to leave a message for me since I didn't have a phone yet. I hadn't been home an hour before my sister was knocking on my door, yelling and telling me I had to call this number back right away. It was the EFNEP committee and they had been so impressed with my interview that they decided not to interview any further. The job was mine if I wanted it. Thank you God! There were some changes: (1) this was a part-time position and (2) I would not be teaching adults, but would be teaching children for the youth component of the EFNEP program. This program worked hand-in-hand with Ingham County Cooperative Extension and Michigan State University. My wages would be partially funded from each agency. It was indeed, my most rewarding job ever.

I had found a house, got a job with Michigan State University and found a church home all within a month. Things were falling in place rapidly for me. I worked hard and was soon traveling across the state providing workshops and developing programs. It may have been a part-time job, but I was working full time. I had enrolled back in school and took the State of Michigan exam. I checked off every job they had that I thought I could do. My testing lasted all day. I was so excited when I received my results and saw that I passed with high scores in every area. My lowest score in 15 different areas was a 92%. It was not long before I started getting letters to interview for different positions. I really wanted a job in data entry but they weren't hiring. I was called in to take another math test and after the test one of the interviewers called me in to ask if I would please consider working in Individual Income Taxes. I had a family and this was full time work with the best benefits ever. I took the job.

I audited taxes for two years before they transferred me to Problem Resolutions. This area was protected and closed off for employee safety. I was told it was because of my temperament that I was asked to work in that unit. Nobody wanted to deal with the upset and mostly irritated people on the other end of the phones. It didn't really bother me and I usually could calm them down and assure them that I only wanted to be a help to them. When I couldn't do that, I just asked them to call us back when they felt better. I worked in that unit for another three years before I saw an opportunity to upgrade for a better paying position in the Department of Education. I interviewed for the position with the National School Lunch Program which was a federally funded program, so I was working for the State of Michigan and the Federal Government at the same time. The pay and benefits were good and God was still working on my behalf. I was able to work there with the National School Lunch Program for the next eleven years until I retired!

I call this a Survivor's Story because a few years after I joined my church my pastor's wife asked me if I would be a part of a panel of women who didn't mind telling their story to help other women. I agreed to do it and was asked to talk about being raped. At first I could hardly talk about my stepfather or the man who raped me as an adult without crying. However, I knew some women needed to know that they could live after rape. I gathered as much material as I could find and put together packets for the women who wanted them. They were filled with information about what to expect and where to go for help. The most amazing thing about it all was the more I shared my story, the more healing I received. I still get a bit emotional sometimes when I talk about it, but NOT every time because I am a SURVIVOR!

All I could do was *pray!*

Inspirational Thoughts

The innocence of your youth can be damaged. The effect will last through a lifetime if not properly addressed. There are many predators who rob the innocence of children. The long-term effects of childhood sexual abuse have been correlated with higher levels of depression, guilt, shame, self-blame, eating disorders, somatic concerns, anxiety, dissociative patterns, repression, denial, sexual problems, and relationship problems. The witness never received treatment for her abuse. There are many victims around you. Your mother, sister, best friend, brother, father, or even your child could be a victim. They silently walk amongst you everyday.

The Most High God kept His arms of protection around the witness throughout her difficulties. God instilled in her how to survive and she did. You could always say what you would have done if you were in that situation. It's easier said than done. She was abused during her childhood and throughout her marriage. Do you think a person can get accustomed to suffering, accustomed to mistreatment, and accustomed to disrespect? What about you? How does this testimony makes you feel? Do you feel compassion or anger?

The witness only needed to believe in her capabilities, release her fears, and to trust God. Fear of the 'what ifs' held her captive. Once she believed in her heart and in God, she knew the rest would be up to her. When you make one step, God will make the rest for you. You must help yourself and believe in yourself in order to elevate yourself. You have the ability to change your situation because you are a child of The Most High God. He sent His son Jesus for you so you know He loves you unconditionally. Love yourself! If you look in the mirror and don't love the image you see then change how you see the image.

It's your life. Release your fears, take your leap of faith with Jesus; He is your protection. Tomorrow is not promised. The witness realized she needed to make a change and took a leap of faith. She stopped being a victim and became a survivor to help other victims. Now it's your time to survive and to take your leap of faith. It's time to shred the skin that keeps you bound.

Help is just a phone call away!

Call someone who can help: 800.656.4673
Chat online at: online.rainn.org

RAINN is the nation's largest anti-sexual violence organization. RAINN created and operates the National Sexual Assault Hotline in partnership with more than 1,000 local sexual assault service providers across the country. If you or someone you know has been sexually assaulted, help is available.

Crisis Support Service

Sexual Assault and Harassment
- *National Sexual Assault Hotline: a service of RAINN*
  o *Telephone hotline: 800-656-HOPE (4673)*

- *National Street Harassment Hotline: a service of Stop Street Harassment*
  o *Telephone hotline: 855.897.5910*

- *DoD Safe Helpline: a service for members of the U.S. military and their families, operated by RAINN for the Department of Defense*
  o *Telephone hotline: 877.995.5247*

- *Domestic and Dating Violence*
  o *Telephone hotline: 800.799.SAFE*

- *Love is Respect: a service of the National Domestic
  Violence Hotline*
o *Telephone hotline: 866.331.9474*

Other Victims of Crime
- *Victim Connect: A service of the National Center for Victims
  of Crime for all crime victims*
o *Telephone hotline: 855.4.VICTIM (84-2846)*

- *National Human Trafficking Hotline: a service of Polaris*
o *Telephone hotline: 888.373.7888*

- *National Center for Missing and Exploited Children*
o *Telephone hotline: 800.THE.LOST (843-5678)*

He Heals
The Wounds Of Every
Shattered Heart!

Deuteronomy 31:6

"Be strong and courageous. Do not fear or be in dread of them, for it is the Lord your God who goes with you. He will not leave you or forsake you."

CHAPTER 18

Bustin' Loose
The Miracle of a Transformed Perspective

REV. LEELA BROWN WALLER
Kennesaw, Georgia

*"So, Jesus said to him, unless you see Sighs and Wonders
you will not believe."* John 4:48

Happy New Year, it is the year 2020. My Pastor has decreed and declared that this is the year of God's double favor. However, no one could fathom or imagine how God's glory would be revealed, collectively and individually, in this New Year. Yes, I was expecting God's indescribable double favor.

Just as the little boy in the Clorox bleach TV commercial cries out, "Mom I have a situation," I found myself at my bedside in early March crying out that same sentiment, "Lord we have a situation." The lock down was real. Coronavirus, also known as COVID-19, had captured our land. A virus that many had no idea of the crucial devastation it would bring. The World had never been here before in our lifetime. Lives were being affected by sickness and death. After praying I had encountered an inner peace and stillness knowing that the Lord was in control. I embraced the word of God found in Psalm 46:10 "Be still and know I am God." I was acknowledging who God is and that I was covered by the blood of Jesus.

Most people thought what started in March surely would be over or controlled by the summer. Truly the hot summer heat would kill the virus, and yes, we would be back in full swing, going to our favorite summer hangouts, beaches, jazz concerts and most of all, back in the walls of the church. As a servant of God, surely I would be back doing the Lord's work of ministry. Sadly, COVID-19 had no regard for the summer season. Not only was COVID-19 taking possession of breath, but a social unrest was in effect brought on by the killing of George Floyd at the hands of police, where his voice cried out, "I can't breathe." The year 2020 had become the year of finding our breath.

In the first week of July, I was able to find a job in the middle of this COVID-19 pandemic, what a miracle. The only requirements were to pass a test and obtain my State Health License in a week. Now that was crazy because this test, training and preparation takes months. Just to let you know I deal in crazy because I have a crazy God. "For nothing is impossible with God" Luke 1:31. At the same time I was preparing to preach virtually that upcoming Sunday to the congregation and to the world via the internet.

My God, I was so focused on the assignments God had put before me. Hallelujah, I studied for four days, passed the test on Friday, and preached on Sunday. I preached a powerful sermon titled "Bustin' Loose," my scripture was John 11:40-44, the story of Lazarus being raised from the dead. The Bible said, "Loose him and Let him go." In that preaching moment, I was led by the Holy Spirit to deliver a prophetic Word to his people.

Here's what I uttered in a passionate voice: "Somehow, someway in the middle of our situation, God is saying I need you who believe in me to Bust Loose."

Can I tell you that miracles are happening right now! Do not get it twisted God is still on the throne. Yes, many have died and many have been sacrificed in the name of COVID-19. But those of you who have their minds on Jesus need to focus on God's Signs and Miracles for your life. Whether it is healing, a new job, a new revelation about

God or a revelation of where you will spend Eternity.

If you want to **Bust Loose** it starts with a right **Mindset**.

A Mindset– that God is still in control. If COVID-19 takes me out or here I've got another house not built by Man, but by God.
A Mindset– of the battle has been fought and victory has been won, we are Winners.
A Mindset– greater is He that's in me than he that's in the World.
A Mindset– that there is no stopping us now. Yes, in the midst of this dark season, God is calling us to trust Him and Bust Loose.

In my mind I was in a good space, the space where God wanted me to be. I had proclaimed to myself and others that, "I'm Bustin' Loose."

Little did I know that God desired a higher level for me in Him, I was not where God wanted me to be. A miracle was about to take place for me to really move into an amazing perspective and live in a place of God's glory. On that afternoon after God used me, I was exposed to COVID-19 by a good friend at lunch. My friend became sick and was admitted into the hospital that Tuesday and diagnosed with COVID-19. On the next day while on the COVID floor, I spoke with him and we had prayer. I knew then that I was infected with the virus; however, I tried self and home medication to boost my immune system. By the next week I could not hold my head up out of bed, I knew it was time to call 911.

I was taken to the emergency room, admitted and diagnosed with COVID-19. I stayed in the hospital for a week. Although I was weak, I was able to walk. I was treated and released in order to go home and recuperate. By this time, my friend was worse and had been placed on a ventilator.

All was going well until three days later. As I rose that morning the room begin to spin and I found no life in my legs. I crawled on the floor and at some points it seemed as if I was on the ceiling. I was up choking on green mucus and could not breathe. I just knew I was dying. I sat in the middle of the floor calling on the Lord and asked

Him not to let me die alone. In the middle of all this it seemed like my spirit stood still and had a conversation with God. He told me to tell people to breathe. He said, "Some people are breathing but do not recognize that it's my breath. You do not need anyone's applause but mine. No one has a Heaven or Hell to put you in."

God said that we all are going to transition out of this life, however, only what you do for me matters. Your purpose is all about me. What a new perspective I had. God spared my life for His purpose and glory. Having a stroke due to COVID-19 kept me in the hospital for over two weeks with treatment and physical therapy. While in the hospital my friend died along with one other friend of his. I learned that a group of veteran friends had gotten together for a fellowship and that was the hotspot.

Some would say the miracle is that I lived. Yes, I praise God and give thanks to Him everyday for sparing me. However, the transformation of my perspective (how I see things), my consciousness (how I think), and how I exist was the miracle that I needed in order to truly bust loose into my God's purpose here on earth. If I was going to really live and have a prophetic relationship with God, I had to be all His, trusting and moving in Christ as his daughter. Not only are the miracles in God's written Word that we may believe, His Miracles in our experiences also moves us to higher levels in believing that Jesus is the Christ, the Son of God.

Breathe...

• Prayer•

I pray that each of you who read these words will Bust Loose in God's purpose for your lives. I pray that you will not look for anyone's applause but God's. I pray that you will love others as you love yourself. I declare and decree that because God is powerful that you too will walk in power. Most of all please recognize that God is your Creator and that his breath is what you breathe. I praise God for all his Miracles, and remember that you are a Miracle.

Amen!

I embraced the **word** *of God!*

Maxine Williams Wright

Inspirational Thoughts

A great number of people had high expectations for 2020, the year of double favor. The Most High God heard the declarations, but there was something else brewing in the pot for 2020. The year was beyond anything that could be imagined. The year brought about death, unemployment, foreclosures, businesses closing, isolation, and shut downs. Panic was throughout the globe because the virus did not have any restrictions. It has been a time to be still and develop a closer relationship with The Most High God. It has been a time to be grateful if you can breathe and a time to be obedient.

Since the virus, ask yourself:
1) Do you see without judgment?
2) Do you listen wholeheartedly?
3) Do you speak truth?
4) Do you walk in faith?
5) Do you worship for real?

Before the pandemic there were many hordes of zombies who did not care who they devoured, or who they destroyed or who they changed. During this crisis you would think there would be more love and compassion. But hate holds the number one position and is streaming live everywhere.

Do you think God is trying to tell you something? Do you think God is trying to get your attention? The witness determined God had a message for her. What message have you received during this pandemic? What has The Most High God spared you from? Whatever it might be, just stop and praise Him. God knew this was going to happen and I'm grateful for the breath He allows me to breathe. Are you grateful? Do you allow your light to shine for all to see just how glorious Jesus can be? He came so we may breathe! He came to mend, to tend, and to blend!

Are you ready to bust loose in God's purpose for your life. Listen closely! Be still! Pay attention! Now breathe the double favor of The Most High God! Arise in your new beginning!

Just Breathe And Pray!

James 1:2-4

"Consider it pure joy, my brothers and sisters, whenever you face trials of many kinds, because you know that the testing of your faith produces perseverance. Let perseverance finish its work so that you may be mature and complete, not lacking anything."

Maxine Williams Wright

CHAPTER 19

Faith vs. Reality

DOROTHY D. HART
Douglasville, Georgia

When we think of Faith versus reality what comes to mind? In a world of multi-ethnic groups with demographic formalities, cultural backgrounds, and spiritual beliefs, I'm sure we could come up with a tsunami of responses. Overwhelming to think of right, maybe just your only thought would be enough. Some of us may not have considered the world we live in. If you've managed to live from day to day you've had to have faith over your reality. We cannot refuse to love the truth that faith exists and it is present in most of our realities.

In our world today, failure is almost the unpardonable sin. Our success is idolized, and idolized success is a picture of the fear of grace. The fear of grace causes pressure that creates major stress, deceit, and lies from people. As long as we are following the ways of the world, we will move toward brokenness and death rather than God's grace and life. The world wages war against our souls. There are forces that cause people to drift away from God. The flesh, the world, and the devil are the enemies of our faith and grace which should be our reality. God's grace is greater than these. Our Faith is the complete confidence and trust in God and His Grace. God's grace is all sufficient, more than enough for all we will ever need. God may not always deliver us from the fire but He will walk through the fire with us. God has not called us to be independent but to be dependent on Him through faith.

Our simple minds cannot commit to governmental law without having faith. We know that the root of the matter is that the law of God is supreme with all the choices we have to make in our lives. We have to submit to God to cooperate with our spirit. This helps us to be free to help ourselves and help other people maneuver in this society. This society is our reality we have to embrace it from a spiritual perspective to encounter the process that drives us to our destiny. I encourage you to resist the mindset of depending on your own abilities or what you can do for yourself.

Grace is Jesus Christ himself showing up whether you're in faith or in the reality stage. There is no grace apart from Him. There is no faith apart from what you believe. It is grace at the beginning and grace at the end. There is enough grace issued from God's throne for us to cope with all the sorrows, the heartaches, the difficulties, the temptations, the Pandemic and the trials we face. To fully embrace your faith life is to fully embrace your own need of God's grace. It is by grace we have been saved. This is not from ourselves; it is the gift of God, not by works so that no one can boast. For we are God's handiwork, created in Christ Jesus to do good works which God prepared in advance for us to do. (Ephesians 2:8-10)

We've been in situations where we had to make it and we needed God to prove his power to us. We've spent time trying to figure out a situation on our own only to realize that we had to depend on God to get it done. Faith does not mean that things won't happen to you. Sometimes things had to happen for us to get to the level of faith needed for the process to be completed. Yes, faith propels us to the next level. It changes our minds and encourages us to trust the process not the circumstances we're in. We all must go through moments of doubt misery, heartache and pain. It's just a season of your life where you have to decide "What must I do while I'm in this position?" Perseverance is what it takes for us to achieve in life. We have to go through experiences and endure during the pressure.

Remember, rare and precious diamonds have been pressurized over time to become the finest. This is a learned experience of my own.

In the midst of many failed situations I found out that I needed to overcome these circumstances to get where God wanted and needed me to be. Every struggle I had to endure brought pain. I decided that I can't stay there. I asked, "Lord what must I do with this? How can I take my mistakes and turn them into a miracle?" He answered, "Trust me with your assignment." It was then I learned that situations I've gone through weren't about me. It's about the gift God had in store for me. After my foreclosure I learned that my desires are not God's desire for me. It had to happen. Once I put God at the forefront of my desires He gave me the above and beyond. And no man can take credit for what God has done. When I was in the middle of the storm it seemed like there was no end. I've been in a place where I had to have friends come forth on my behalf to help me sustain. It was then I realized that if God allowed it, it had to happen. Every mistake made had to take place because God needed me just where I am right now.

Even being a victim of a humiliating broken marriage was a celebrated process. It was there where I realized the magnitude of a fool's mentality can't win. It was there where the brokenness helped me to know that God Himself is my secure place. I had to trust God's purpose for my life more than the reality where I found myself. Having someone tell you that you can't eat at your own dinner table was debilitating to my being. Finding yourself working late at night to avoid going home was depressing. I realized that I had to break free because the devil wanted to smother me from serving God. I had to realize that the place God prepared for me was not there. In all this, God allowed me to see a door of peace.

Jesus will destroy the chains that bind you.

I know that in this world we appear as strange fruit hanging for picking. Picked out to be picked on. However, if we stay in faith God will provide. We have a powerful spiritual weapon which is in the "Name of Jesus." We are saved by His name, "for there is no other name under Heaven given among men by which we must be saved." (Acts 4:12) The dark spiritual world knows that power and authority of Jesus' name and it trembles. His name is a powerful weapon because it represents all that Jesus accomplished both in the natural realm here on earth as well as in the spiritual world. "God has highly exalted Him and given Him the name which is above every name, that at the name of Jesus every knee should bow." (Philippians 2:9) Choose wisely who you will travel with and the road you will travel, for it will lead you to your final destination. Instead of seeing difficult times as reasons to doubt God's love, see them as faith adventures. Your faith in God connects you to His sovereign power. Nothing and no one can separate you from God's love. There is power in the name of Jesus! Receive it and use it.

Often time there are things that seem to isolate you but do not allow these things to get in your head. God has a plan of rescue for your mind. Sometimes there are family matters that conflict us emotionally and personally. The disobedient child that tries to undermine your love as a parent. The loss of love ones back to back. The abuse of power on the job. These occurrences cause us to isolate from others and don't allow us to properly process the transition of the hurt and pain that's transpiring. I've been through more pain than people can imagine but I never gave up. No matter what transpired I had to remain kind and honest. However, when someone tries to stop me and bring me down I turned into a lioness that cannot be tamed. I knew God was up to something. You have to remain compassionate about what you believe and your goals. Smile on your bad days. Never stop and push until you prevail. This requires strong faith in the reality of the fight. Don't be tamed in your circumstances.

As God's people we are called to speak that which honors Him. Death and life are in the power of the tongue. Words can create or destroy; they can uplift or condemn. They can reflect the word by which God has spoken, or they can echo the whispers of satan. We live in a world with a vast and unlimited economy of words. Today, there are more ways to communicate than at any time in human history. Social media has become the whereto say whatever with no filters and very little truths. But one way you can commit to truth telling online is by pausing before you engage, especially with posts that seem hard to believe. Sometimes the best way to commit to the truth is to seek discernment which often dictates you to say nothing at all. "Even a fool is considered wise when he keeps silent, discerning, when he seals his lips." (Proverbs17:28) As Christians our speech should be truthful. Truthful speech is the sign of a redeemed heart that avoids lying. Lying is a sin, the work of the enemy, and the product of a fallen nature. Proverbs 12:22-23 ESV says, "Lying lips are detestable to the Lord, but faithful people are his delight. A shrewd person conceals knowledge, but a foolish heart publicizes stupidity." Kindness, respect, and good manners are considered Christian virtues. Hatred stirs up conflicts but love covers all offenses. "God resists the proud, but gives Grace to the humble." Words matters! Be a "tree of life" to others.

I said all that to say that "I've been lied on, cheated, abused, evicted, fired, broken, hurt, depressed, confused, manipulated, challenged, broke financially, married, divorced, betrayed, disrupted, disrespected, tried, shamed, envied, attacked, wrongfully accused, hated, embarrassed and misunderstood. In the midst of all of that I had to realize that death and life were in the power of my tongue. I had to allow God to transform my thinking. I used the word of God to paint the picture of my success. Daily concentration and quiet time with God worked for me. I focused on Philippians 4:8, "Finally brethren, whatsoever things are true, whatsoever things are honest, whatsoever things are just, whatsoever things are pure, whatsoever things are lovely, whatsoever things are of good report; if there be any virtue and if there be any praise think on these things." With that discipline I can now say that I am prosperous and successful in my life which covers complete wholeness in every area. I couldn't have done it without God's Grace, utilizing strong Faith in the midst of my reality. Your reality can shift when the tools you use are orchestrated by God. You have to tap into your inner being to adapt to God's way of doing things. Be still and know that God is God. There were many days and nights I thought I should be crying but something wouldn't allow me to cry. It didn't feel like a hardened heart. That's when I knew God was doing a new thing in me. No matter what happened to me, around me and about me, I always think that God is in charge. My faith had a comfort of peace in my heart which shielded me from all the stuff taking place in my life. I managed my disappointment by allowing God to be in total control. I had to let go of my total will and take on God's will for my life. I had to change my habits to align with God's word, which created a totally different person from inside out. I felt like Super Woman. I believed I could even when I didn't know how I would. My testimony is, "God did it all."

In conclusion, "Do not love this world nor the things it offers you, for when you love the world, You do not have the love of the Father in you." (1Jonh 2:15) We see in this world, people like what they have always known. Changes disrupt their routine and move people out of their comfort zone so they disagree and resist. Changes cannot be forced with power and authority. Power is not based on physical, intellectual, social, economic, or political superiority. Power is expressed in service, and in weakness. Jesus turned the world upside down, not with force but with service. He influenced and demonstrated this through His life. The ways of the world are to take the quick and easy way to the top, but there is no shortcut. God's way is by having faith in the midst of your reality. Trust God in all your ways and have integrity with all your actions.

Dorothy D. Hart, Author
Personal and Professional Lifestyle Coach
Dorothy Hart Enterprises, LLC
info@dorothydhart.com & www.dorothydhart.com

God did it **all!**

Inspirational Thoughts

As you live in this world you must know it is only by God's grace that you exist. Have you ever wondered why some people prosper and others do not? That's how this world has programmed you to think. The individuals with money, fame, degrees, and titles are the ones this world considers prosperous. There's nothing wrong with those things. Society tends to reduce your creditability if not in a certain income bracket, if not residing in a certain neighborhood, if not a member of a certain sorority/fraternity, if not a certain skin tone, if not an alumni of a certain school, if not wearing designer clothes, if not driving a certain make and model car, if not having a certain GPA, and if not physically fit.

Jesus was born in a manger. Jesus was a carpenter. Jesus had no address. Jesus was a King without an earthly castle, yet He sits on His heavenly throne besides His Father. Jesus had no interest in worldly possessions, He came to serve. Are you willing to serve? Will you follow Jesus?

You must not compare yourself to anyone because you are purposely designed. You must not allow anyone to invalidate who you are; no one has power over you. The same people that try to judge you are the same people struggling with their own battles. People of the world create raging battles not knowing they are puppets of dark forces. By being of this world how will you change this world?

You must have a relationship with The Most High God to have a spirit of discernment. You must be able to know when to fold your hand or play your hand. Allow the Spirit of Jesus to go before you to clear the grounds, to rid thy enemies, to cast out ungodly spirits, to fight your battles.

The witness came to terms with her reality. She chose to travel her road with The Most High God. She realized the power of her tongue. Do know the power of your tongue? The tongue has no bones, but is strong enough to break hearts. Do you speak life over your life? Speak precisely!

Schedule your service appointment for grace, favor and lifetime protection. Get ready for the alignments in your heart, mind, and tongue!

Isaiah 40:31

"But those who hope in the Lord will renew their strength. They will soar on wings like eagles; they will run and not grow weary, they will walk and not be faint."

Maxine Williams Wright

CHAPTER 20

Removed From the List

MAXINE WILLIAMS WRIGHT
Marietta, Georgia

The Founder's Day program was different in 2019 when the committee chose to recognize the women of the college. The institution showed appreciation to the dedicated women that stayed the course through it all. Somehow three members of the committee decided not to include me. When I received the news I was heartbroken. I had been employed since 2001 and endured the struggles and the financial hardships through the loss of accreditation in 2003. Student enrollment reduced drastically after the loss which caused a massive layoff. The remaining faculty and staff became accustomed to no compensation on payroll due dates.

I eventually depleted my retirement funds and savings. Many devoted faculty members and staff stayed the course to ensure the doors of the college would remain open. They, too, depleted their funds and some lost their cars and homes. I often worked part-time at other companies to have some type of income since I was single, but I always made sure there was time to work my part-time hours at the college without receiving compensation. Finally, I started working a full-time position in 2015 after I prayed to the Most High God to keep me from going back to having nothing. I still worked my part-time hours at the college in the evenings and weekends to ensure my responsibilities were completed. I sat numb during the service as I thought about the many years I managed three departments (Human Resources, Payroll, and Facilities) without any additional compensation for the sake of the school. As I sat there I thanked God for keeping me through it all. There was no doubt in my mind that He was indeed with me. But I just didn't understand why I was not included on the list with the other women. I asked God to give me strength as I sat through the program and to keep the north Memphis side of me composed.

I sat there and thought about the sacrifices I had made through the years and the opportunities I allowed to go by while refusing to give up on the college. The foreclosure notice I received during my tenure made it real and I had no choice but to get a fulltime job. Sometimes you have to get slapped in the face to wake from a daze. My eyes were wide open then so I contacted the mortgage company to apply for a loan modification but it wasn't approved due to my part-time wages. All they wanted to know was when I was going to pay my mortgage. At that point I drifted back into a comatose state and continued my normalcy. There was nothing else I knew to do because I couldn't shutdown. I couldn't allow myself to get depressed. I knew the possible outcome.

It happened when I was in my late twenties. My second husband was upset because I wouldn't reconcile with him. He came to my apartment and took items I had managed to take with me when I left him. My niece was living with me at the time and deescalated the situation. I cried all night after he left. I went to work the next day and felt some kind of way about the night before. I went to use the ladies room and as I washed my hands I looked intensely in the mirror at the reflection but didn't recognize the face. The person within didn't match the reflection. It seemed as if the image was not real and the real person wanted to get out. I could no longer pretend and no longer smile when there was so much pain inside. I screamed and screamed to release my anger, my pain, my hurt, and my disappointment. I slid down the wall to the floor. My manager came in and sat on the floor with me. He wrapped his arms around me and rocked me. He stayed on the floor with me until I was calm.

I only remember hearing a gentle voice that soothed my spirit. I don't ever want to have an episode like that again. I couldn't stress about my financial challenges; I did the best I could do, and at that point I didn't worry about it. As our ancestors would say, "You can't get blood out of a turnip." I just felt in my spirit The Most High God was not going to allow me to be homeless. He had brought me too far.

The mortgage company called often, so I decided not to accept their calls. They only caused more stress to an already stressful situation which I couldn't allow. I managed to make enough on my part-time job to pay my car note every other month and to keep the utilities from being disconnected. I monitored the utilities and kept the bill amounts low. The house was hot in the summer and cold in the winter. Most summer nights were restless due to the heat and winter nights I used plenty of blankets with a space heater.

I trusted God enough to know even if I lost my home and landed in a ditch, I would be okay as long as He was with me. Months went by without me answering the mortgage company's phone calls and one day they just stopped calling. I didn't know what to expect, so I continued to stay active at church with the Drama Ministry. I kept busy in order not to have room to worry. My youngest son often got upset with me for giving rides to cast members. During a production I felt obligated to make sure they got to rehearsal and got back home. One day my son said, "Why do you continue to drive up and down the street picking up folks and taking them home when you don't have gas money? The gas money I gave was for you to use and not for them." My response was this, "At least I have transportation, they don't."

My son didn't say anything else to me about giving people rides. But I stopped giving rides to men I really didn't know when one of the ministers at church called a meeting with me to discuss just how dangerous that could possibly be. I was obedient and only gave rides to men I knew. For some reason I had a soft spot in my heart for black men that encountered hardships. From raising two sons on my own in Cobb County, I understood their struggles and sympathized with them. I witnessed the injustice in the judicial system, the unfairness with employers, and the veil stamped across their faces for being Black Men. I stayed on my knees for my sons. Thank God for His protection and grace.

God sent redemption to His people.

After I obtained a full-time position, I strategically planned to set funds aside to present to the mortgage company. That position was a gift from God when I answered the third call from an employer. I knew the mortgage company would require a lump sum for the arrears. The plan was in motion but I just needed a little more time. Every evening I entered the subdivision not knowing what I would find. When I turned on my street I prayed not to see my belongings on the curbside. Thank You God was all I could say each day I came home from work. The house had three levels with five bedrooms, four bathrooms and a finished basement. It was indeed a haven for many souls along the way. My door was opened for family and friends who needed to stay a night and those who needed a place to live. At the time I didn't realize the similarities I had with my mother. I was indeed my mother's daughter. Mom fed and sheltered many throughout her life in her home. She was a jewel when it came to sharing and helping others.

After the death of my father she was alone. We cautioned her to be careful with strangers. That was like talking to the wall. Mom did what mom wanted to do. Mom's sister moved in and we all thought it was great. Mom wouldn't be home alone anymore. As time passed mom's first cousin who was deceased had a daughter that needed a place to live and of course mom allowed her to move-in. My aunt was apprehensive about the idea. "Mom, I don't understand why she came to live with you when she has so many siblings. Something must be wrong when her immediate family won't take her in, please be careful," I stated. My aunt kept me informed on what mom did since I lived in Georgia and they were in Memphis, Tennessee.

Then one day my aunt informed me that my cousin had been disrespectful toward her and believed she was on drugs. So I talked to mom about it and she said, "It's nothing, don't worry about it, everything will be okay." So I had no choice but to let it go and asked mom to be careful and to keep close watch on my cousin. Mom was too trusting! After a few weeks had passed, I received a phone call from a family member informing me my aunt was in ICU. My cousin had stabbed her with a knife over 10 times, choked her with her hands, smothered her with a pillow, then robbed her and left my aunt for dead. My mother and sister found my aunt when they returned from church on a Sunday afternoon. My cousin thought she had killed her, but my aunt was conscious and coherent and reported all the details to the police officers. My mid 70 year old aunt was indeed a blessed woman who survived a horrific act against her. After that tragedy we did not allow mom to take in anyone else. Mom learned that family could sometimes hurt you the most. That was a lesson for us all. We should have cautioned mom about family as well. Praise God my aunt survived and was okay. I also learned from that tragedy and was mindful of persons I allowed in my home. I had faith that The Most High God was making arrangements on my behalf for my home. He was not going to allow me to be homeless. I just felt it.

The consequences of not paying my mortgage for a year marinated throughout my entire body. The night before I planned to make the call was indeed a restless night. While at work the next day I took a break and went to a secluded area. I took deep breaths as I called the mortgage company. The customer service representative needed my personal information. When she retrieved my file I told her I was ready to make payment arrangements. I asked about the foreclosure, the allotted timeframe to get caught up, and the amount I had to pay. She stated, "Your home is not under foreclosure." At that point I was confused. Then I mentioned the notice I had received in the mail months ago. The representative said, "Your home was on the list, then your home was removed from the list."

I didn't quite understand, my head started to spin and I leaned against a wall and said, "Thank You God!" I got myself together and asked about the amount I needed to pay to get caught up. Representative responded, "Just your scheduled mortgage payment and I will put the debt owed on the backend." My eyes filled with praise, my heart leaped with joyfulness, and my mind absorbed His greatness! Right at that moment I knew The Most High God removed my name from the list of foreclosures.

The Most High God had once again interceded on my behalf. His miraculous plan! His process tuned my character, fashioned my perspectives, extended my endurance, and instilled me with strength. At the end of the Founder's Day program I was no longer upset with the committee members that chose not to include me on their list. I couldn't allow bitterness to fill my spirit; God had been too good to me.

The Most High God has the power to remove your name and to arrange your name. He knows what list you should be on and what list you should not be on. Just make sure your name is on God's list! Does He know your name?

I trusted *God*
enough to know

even if...

Maxine Williams Wright

Inspirational Thoughts

When I think about His goodness
It takes me to a time
Was down to my last dime
There were situations I couldn't handle
Wanted to throw in the towel, yell surrender
Yet, He reminded me of all the countless possibilities meant to be
All unforeseen talents waiting to be released.

Angels
around you and Love that
surrounds you Stretch forth
your wings and fly!

CPSIA information can be obtained
at www.ICGtesting.com
Printed in the USA
BVHW050831190522
637504BV00010B/87